AM I THE ASSHOLE

By Jamie Goldson

1.THE GUITAR

This occurred quite some time ago. Even after all this time, my wife and I still talk about it every now and then. She, as well as the majority of our friends and family, are on my side. Nonetheless, when the incident occurred, it was like World War III between us and her co-workers and others.

For the past 22 years, I've been playing the guitar. I'm well-versed in the intricacies of guitar values and so on. I'm extremely interested in the guitar market. When my wife was working at her earlier company, she was hanging out with co-workers one evening after work when she mentioned that I should play guitar for them. A co-worker, who I assume is very popular at work, informed me that his father had passed away and that he was selling his father's belongings. His father had a guitar and had inquired with my wife about whether I would be interested in buying it. My wife sent me a text, and I responded by telling him to send me the information about the guitar and the price. The following day, he texted me the pictures and the price. It turned out to be a 1952 Telecaster in excellent condition. He had the original receipts, which was incredible! (It was from these receipts that I was able to decide the date.) "I looked up telecasters online and he believes $4,000 is a reasonable price," he explained when I inquired about his asking price. I responded with a text saying, "I'll take it for $4,000," and then went to pick it up. He didn't care about the guitar because it held no sentimental value for him.

The problem at hand is as follows: I was well aware that the guitar was worth approximately $50,000, depending on the buyer, and I was prepared to pay for it. When I received the guitar, I informed my wife of the purchase price and the value of the instrument. She was completely taken aback. Fast forward two weeks, and her co-worker informs my wife that he recently discovered how much the guitar was actually worth from a family friend and that he wishes to have it returned. She expressed herself as follows: "He really likes the guitar, and he was aware that it was worth $50,000, which is why he was taken aback when you offered it to him for $4,000 instead of $50,000. I really like it, and I don't think he'll sell it back to you, but you can always ask him. " (This was probably not the best thing for her to say, but she was caught off guard and it is not her fault or problem.) He got in touch with me and asked if he could buy it back. I made it clear that it was not for sale. In response, he said that I had scammed him and that he would "sue me and take my wife to HR for being a part of the scam." which was absurd, but he did, in fact, contact human resources. They were unconcerned about it and said that it was not their concern. It's a one-on-one battle between him and me. His actions at work made my wife's working environment extremely uncomfortable over the next few months. He would pester her about it on a regular basis. Finally, she had to report him to HR for harassment, and they actually let him go (she complained twice, and he was warned twice more, but still didn't stop.) He's contacted me about it several times, and I've filed a restraining order against him for harassment as well. I, too, had him blocked. I haven't heard back from him in over a year and a half.

Am I the Asshole?

2.THE REWARD AND THE CAT

This past weekend, while walking through the park, I came across a cat that looked similar to the one I had seen on posters that had been posted around the neighbourhood earlier in the year. In exchange for finding their missing cat, they offered a $500 reward. Then I caught the cat, which was relatively easy because he was friendly, and verified that it was indeed him by looking at a poster, which turned out to be correct.

I returned home, placed him on the back porch, and dialled the phone number listed on the poster to notify the owners that their cat had been discovered. Their delight at having found him led to their offering to have him picked up at once afterward. As soon as I found out that there was a $500 reward, I texted the guy with a picture of the cat and my mailing address.

This is the point at which the difficulty begins. The moment he arrived at my residence, I demanded payment for the cat's return before returning him to his home. It was later revealed that there was no reward and that he only advertised one in order to increase the likelihood that people would seek out his cat. When he refused to pay the promised reward, I told him that he shouldn't have posted one in the first place and that he should have known that I wouldn't return his cat until he paid. I refused to give him the cat, and he became angry and threatened to call the authorities. I told him that he was welcome to do so and that I would be delighted to get things on the record in the event that I needed to take him to small claims court later on. His words were tepid, and he promised that he would return with the money later. It was resolved later that night when he came by with the full $500 and I returned his cat to him.

So am I the Asshole?

She thought I should have just given the cat back to him because it had cost me nothing to catch him and because everyone was going through tough times at the time. When I told my girlfriend about it, she agreed with her. My friends also believe that the man was probably desperate to get his pet back and that it was a little shady of me to make money off of a misplaced dog. I still believe that if you post a reward, you should honour it, and that the guy was most likely just looking to save $500 while also reaping the benefits of advertising a reward without having to pay for it himself.

So, am I the Asshole?

3.THE MISTRESS AND HER CHILD

Many friends and family members are unaware of this because it is a difficult subject to discuss with anyone I actually know about. In the hopes that someone here will be able to provide me with an honest response, I'm posting on an alternate forum.

Approximately 6 months elapsed between the time I married my husband of 10 years and the affair. We went to couple's counselling and other things after I discovered what he was doing. However, it was discovered that the woman was pregnant and wanted to keep the child. When she told me she was pregnant, I understood that my husband would have to contribute financially to that child's upbringing (at the very least, financially).

Unfortunately, the baby died as a result of the birth. Not only was I not looking forward to this baby's arrival, but I also did not want this. Funeral arrangements have been sent to me by my husband's former lover. I believe he should not be present. Despite the fact that he had never met this child, he was not even present at the hospital when everything happened. Naturally, if this was the case with a child, he was familiar with, my perspective would be different. For the time being, I am not comfortable with him being released from custody. On the spur of the moment, he suggested that I go along with him. It doesn't work that way. In order to avoid making the woman and her family feel uncomfortable, I will not be attending the funeral. No matter how much I despise her, I will not interfere with her bereavement.

There are only a few people in the family who are aware of the situation. My mother-in-law, my husband's sister, and my mother-in-law According to his sister, the funeral is something he should attend. My mother recommends that I file for divorce if he leaves. Mother in law has made it clear that they will not comment on the situation.

To be honest, I'm at a loss for what to do next. Considering the circumstances, am I making a mistake?

So am I the asshole?

4.THE JOURNEY TO ATHENS

I'm 17 years old and have always wanted to visit the city of Athens. So much so that I taught myself to speak Greek (both standard and Cypriot), as well as to read Ancient Greek, because I adore the country and its people. I have read the Iliad, the Odyssey, and many of Homer's books. It is also in Greek that I watch television, sports, movies, and play video games, and it is with Greek friends online that I do all of this in Greek. When my parents announced that they would be taking us on a family vacation to Athens, I was overjoyed because I have Greek friends in Athens, Thessaloniki, and Lanarca that I wanted to meet up with. As a matter of fact, this would be my first time ever leaving the country on a plane.

This occurred during a fantastic party, but if it were the only time, we had available to travel to Greece, I would have done it, and my friends were understanding of my situation. Everything I wanted to see in Greece was on my list, including Meteora, Olympiakos stadium, the Acropolis, Plaka, and other attractions throughout Athens, as well as possible visits to other cities like Sparta and Thessaloniki if we had time. My top priority was to visit universities in Greece because that is where I want to pursue my academic career. This is something I showed my parents, and they responded with, "Yeah, you can do that, we don't mind."

According to the itinerary, the trip will take place in February. My assumption was that we would be stopping in Atlanta. We arrive at the airport, and my parents inform me that we must get to the hotel and that we will need a car rental. Strange, but whoever or whatever wasn't paying attention was in trouble.

After about an hour of driving, I fall asleep in the car, and when we arrive in Athens, Georgia, my parents say, "Hey, we're here, wake up sleepy head," and I notice a sign that reads, "Welcome to Athens, Georgia." My sister bursts out laughing, and my father bursts out laughing as well. We're going on a vacation to Athens, Georgia, to my father's friend's lake house, and I asked them if this was a joke, and they said no.

Throughout my entire life, I have never been more enraged. At a gas station, I got into a fight with my parents, and they were not pleased. My parents told me that I was an unruly brat and that I should be grateful that they were taking us on vacation. This is the best they could do because they said they couldn't afford to take me to Europe. When I found out that I had missed my friend's birthday party for this boring ass trip in the middle of nowhere Georgia, I declared them liars. It had seemed like a joke to everyone else, and I had no idea what was going on. Naturally, my parents are constantly yelling at me, calling me a brat. I've told them to leave, and I've elbowed the car window several times in my rage, breaking it but also injuring myself in the process.

Because I ran away from home and got on an Atlanta-bound bus, my parents are pleading with me to return home. I told them to fuck off and called a friend of mine who used to attend my school but now attends a university in Atlanta to tell him what was going on. His girlfriend picked me up, and I've been staying with her since school was cancelled in Missouri a few days later. Rather than being furious, my parents are now worried. They have begged me to return home, but I have refused.

15

So Am I the Asshole?

5. DRESSING CASUALLY

It has been nearly a year since I (21Male) began dating my girlfriend (19Female). She is currently pursuing a career as a fashion designer in the United Arab Emirates. In my family, which includes my mother (47Female) (relevant), my mother is a fashion designer.

When my girlfriend invited me to meet her parents last December, she instructed me to "dress nicely" and to remove my ear piercings (her parents are conservative), which I initially refused to do, but ultimately decided to do so in order to make a good first impression. The evening with her parents was pleasant, and everything went smoothly without a glitch.

As part of a recent conversation with my mother, I expressed an interest in introducing my girlfriend to her. She enthusiastically agreed, and I intend to do so sometime next week.

The subject at hand is now the subject of this article. The moment I told my girlfriend about my intention of introducing her to my mother, she became overjoyed and began telling me everything she had in mind for an outfit-all of which, in my opinion, were inappropriate for the occasion due to their revealing nature and the fact that we were only planning on spending a couple of hours in my mother's kitchen talking, rather than going to a fancy restaurant or anything like that. Then I told my girlfriend that, for the reasons said above, she should dress comfortably.

After that, she began telling me about how she really wants to impress my mother with her sense of style and the clothes she makes herself, to which I responded by saying that there would be plenty of opportunities for that to happen in the future.

She said that I was doing the same thing when she asked me to remove my piercing before meeting her parents, to which I responded that she did the same thing when she asked me to change my piercing before meeting her parents, but she said it's not the same. How could I compare removing a piercing to requesting to change her entire outfit? Then she began crying and stormed out of the room, and she is not currently speaking with me anymore.

What if I tell my girlfriend that she should dress more casually? Am I being an asshole?

6. SUNDAYS WITH AN EX

A strange scenario has arisen, and a decision is needed. We have been engaged for almost a year and have been dating for three years before that. I am 32 years old, and Amanda is 34 years old. One of her many children, Alexis, her 12-year-old daughter, is one of many. The bond between me and Alexis is strong. For the most part, my connection with Amanda and her ex-husband is positive. With my new position, I'm completely at ease. The strange thing is that Amanda, her ex-boyfriend, and Alexis are all involved in it. On Sundays, the three of them get together to hang out and talk. After all, it probably began as a family custom that they continued after their divorce. Making breakfast and watching movies with each other is what they do throughout the day. To be honest, I find it somewhat strange. If you want to spend a day a week with your ex, which I don't think is a bad idea, I don't see why you would want to do so. Amanda told me that Alexis looks forward to it every week, so she didn't stop doing it when we first started dating, and I thought it was strange. To begin with, I would simply stay in our room or the basement all day on Sundays. My frustration with being confined to my own home eventually led to my abandoning my home for the majority of the day and travelling elsewhere. No matter where I went, Amanda would never inquire as to my whereabouts. Even if I was gone, they wouldn't notice.

I started out by going to the gym or running errands. Alternatively, I'd go to a pub and get some drinks. But then I reconnected with my old friend Bella, which was a wonderful experience. For five years before becoming good friends, Bella and I were in a relationship for five years. It was only recently that she ended her marriage and moved to a new apartment. One Sunday, I informed her that I was only intending on going to the movies, but she instead invited me over to her house. We smoked some weed, watched some movies, prepared some food, and generally just hung out with one another. Because it was so enjoyable, I've decided to make it a weekly ritual now. I used to go over to Bella's house on Sundays to hang out with her and her friends.

The fact that I hadn't told Amanda about my plans didn't bother me. Each and every Sunday, she never inquired as to my whereabouts or even if she was aware of them. So, Bella came by our house yesterday to drop off my phone charger, which I had forgotten I had left at her apartment the night before. Amanda had inquired as to why Bella had my phone charger in her possession. Moreover, I informed her that this was the location where I had been the previous Sunday. She inquired as to my purpose for being there, and I informed her that it was my usual Sunday hangout location. She had a total meltdown. I expressed my displeasure with myself for not informing her that I was spending time with an ex. "Do you really not see the irony in that statement?" I exclaimed, laughing. She said that this time was different since she was upfront about her and the relationship ex's and that if I had a problem with it, I should have expressed my dissatisfaction sooner. In response, she said that it was something she wanted to bring up with me and that she thought it was essential for her daughter. In order to make myself feel better, was it necessary for me to interfere with the highlight of her daughter's week? Not at all. I'll just sneak out the back door and go to my friend's place. I couldn't understand why this was even a problem in the first place. We have faith in one another and have reached adulthood together. Amanda has informed me that she no longer wants me to spend my Sundays with her and that I should find alternative activities. If that's how we're going to play this, I told you I didn't want your ex over on Sundays anymore.

So am I the asshole?

7. THE FATHER.

As a result of my mother's death when I was very young, my father and I spent a lot of time together, and we were naturally close. He then remarried, this time to my stepmom, whose husband had passed away earlier in the year. Among her four children, I am the youngest by five years and the oldest by one year. I had no objections to my dad getting remarried because I didn't want him to be alone while I was away at college. However, it wasn't that bad for any of the kids because my step-siblings and I kind of viewed the situation as "our parents couldn't be together because of death, so they are with other people because they don't want to be lonely," and they all accepted my dad and I accepted my stepmother. To be clear, I have absolutely no ill will toward my stepmother.

As a rule, I prefer to be alone. I prefer to be alone and prefer to hang out with a small group of individuals rather than a large group of people. My hobbies are also something I want to do alone, as previously said.

Suddenly, everything changed after they moved into our home. The environment is tumultuous, and I feel as if I have no say in anything. In the beginning, my father and stepmother thought it was a terrible idea and had a second room made in the basement, where I was fortunate to be the only one who stayed in my room after some squabbling with my brother. We used to always follow the wishes of my step-siblings because we voted and they always sided with each other. But it was particularly difficult at the time. In fact, even when we went out to dine, we turned off the lights, but they merely picked things they enjoyed together, and I had little influence. Having to live there was a terrible experience. Because it was so loud and I couldn't concentrate on my studies, I received a B and subsequently decided to quit school. Despite the fact that my father and stepmother tried, they felt it was unfair to expect youngsters to stay quiet all of the time.

On one occasion, I had a breakdown and went to my grandparents (my mother's parents) to tell them that I wanted to attend this boarding school that was a feeder for top universities and that I was extremely anxious about my grades. In my letter, I expressed my dissatisfaction with my father and stepmother and said that I had been forced out of my house by my stepbrothers and sister. I mentioned that I was interested in attending this boarding school, and they agreed. When they finally agreed, they told me I would have to phone them twice a week for the rest of the week. And so, it was put together by the professionals.

Currently, I am a student at this institution, and I genuinely miss my home and father. Nonetheless, I do not want to speak to my father because it was his fault that I felt uneasy enough to leave the home where I had spent the majority of my life. My father was a poor parent for placing me in this situation and for choosing the children of another woman over me. I became furious and informed him that he was betraying my late mother by choosing the children of another woman over me. After I was kicked out by my stepmother's children, I told her she should be ashamed of herself. As well as telling her that I would no longer refer to her as my stepmother since she and her family do not deserve the term mother, I informed my father that I would no longer be facetiming him because I would not satisfy him just to reduce his feelings of guilt.

They're both being clingy right now, which makes me question whether I'm the one who's causing all of this trouble!

So am I the asshole?

8. MAKING A LIVING FROM CRAFTING

The past ten years have been spent with my husband, Bob, who is 34 years old, and I (F33). As the sole breadwinner in our household, he bought the property. Since graduating from university, I've pursued additional studies, earning master's and doctoral degrees in the process (My parents paid). When I was finishing up my final year, I became pregnant and gave birth a few months later. The fact that my spouse has always been supportive of me and that we don't reside in a prohibitively expensive place allowed me to pursue my STAHP certification. My family has grown to include three children since then. In exchange for my monthly allowance, Bob has provided me with a variety of small craft projects over the years. The items I was going to make were posted on Facebook during quarantine and received a great response, with people actually wanting to purchase them. As a result, depending on the month, I make anywhere from 4–6K because people seem to appreciate the attention to detail and handcrafted element of the product.

Bob has always been aware of my earnings, but he now believes that I should contribute to the family's home-buying fund. While I'm not opposed to it, my job as a STAHP continues to be full time; I still cook and clean and drop the kids off and pick them up from school; now I just profit from my hobby; he's managed fine all these years; he still makes more than me, so I'm not sure if I should be sharing this, even though technically the monthly money he gave me allowed me to purchase the materials at the outset.

Because I don't want to be unfair to him, I'd like to thank you for your assistance. Although I do not keep all of the money, I have used part of it to enrol the children in extracurricular activities and to purchase a watch that he has been wanting for quite some time. However, I do end up keeping the vast bulk of it.

Because I wasn't working and was still in school when we got married, I'll simply give you some financial information. We do have a prenuptial agreement, and everything he buys and makes belongs to him and no one else's. The children inherit all of his assets and savings, and I inherit 20 percent of his life insurance policy, with the remaining 80 percent going to the children once we pay off the remainder of the mortgage with the proceeds of his estate plan. In order for me to be able to go shopping, he withdraws cash from an account in his name once a month, and I only have one account in which he gives me the "allowance," which is also where my craft money is placed.

So am I the Asshole?

9. THE BULLY

Many of my businesses have been successful, and I've assisted others in doing the same. I'm now influential in a variety of industries in my own state as well as several other states. In addition, I own and run a recruitment firm that is well-known in my state and is also used for internal hiring at my company's headquarters.

During high school, I used to get bullied by a guy named Mark (not his real name). He knew I had OCD and would play games with me in the hopes of causing me to have a breakdown or something. He called me homophobic obscenities while I was going through a bicurious phase. I am also straight. However, I was intentionally bumped in the corridors on a few occasions, though it never got that bad.

In the last few weeks, he has returned to my home state. What is causing this is beyond me; chances are it has something to do with COVID, as is everything these days. Although he has a vague understanding that I own and run businesses, I'm not sure he realises just how much I'm engaged in, how much of the recruitment in my state is done through my agency, or even that I am the owner and operator of that agency!

Several versions of Mark's resume (each tailored to a different field) have recently crossed my desk; to put this in context, I receive a weekly report of all new candidates, with specific people (such as those with job history gaps, which Mark had because each tailored resume had the work experience in the other fields removed) flagged for my approval. As a result, we are able to maintain our position as the leading recruitment agency and continue to attract new clients. All of the fields in which he is interested are ones in which I have a substantial amount of influence.

In case you're wondering, this is how I know he's returned to my state; otherwise, I'm not in touch with my former classmates. My ex-boyfriend has never apologised to me, and from what I can see, he's grown up to be a very typical person who occasionally pokes fun at left-wing political leaders on Facebook but who isn't a conspiracy theorist or anything of that nature.

In my draughts folder right now is an email to all of my business owner friends that essentially says, "bin this guy's resume if it comes past us (recruitment agency) again," as well as a less professional message that says, "this is the guy I told you about from high school. Don't hire him at any cost." I'm debating whether or not to send this message. In my state, if I don't want him to have a decent job, he's unlikely to get one. So, it's not exactly a "worker's economy," but the COVID handling here has been satisfactory.

Being the asshole worries me since returning to your hometown alone often shows that something has gone wrong, and I'm not sure if interfering with his ability to earn a living is the best course of action in that situation. My feelings about what he did to me in high school are likewise mixed. I never felt traumatised or emotionally damaged as a result of it; instead, I was irritated and enraged about it. Is it possible that he's evolved? I can't really ask anyone because no one has kept in touch with him.

To be honest, I don't want him to stay in the state for an extended period of time because I can't tolerate the thought of him being here, and I'm hoping that denying him the opportunity to work would push him out of state. Furthermore, I have a professional reputation to protect, and I do not want him to occupy any positions for any of my client firms if he is the same guy he was in high school, because I believe he will do a poor job and create tension in the workplace.

So am I the asshole?

10. THE BROKEN PROMISE

All of my preparations for college were founded on the promise of financial help from my father, and I applied for early action admission to my preferred college as a result of his promise. Eventually, I was accepted. Due to my father's aid, the cost will be prohibitive, but I will be able to graduate with only a manageable amount of debt.

He told me yesterday that he would be unable to aid me in any way, but that he would be able to aid me in obtaining student loans. I was disappointed. He had told me not to worry about it a month before. My question was, "How did this happen?" He initially tried to dodge the question before admitting that he had put the funds in several stocks and had lost money on them. The money he promised me was 70,000 dollars. However, he only had about 32,000 dollars in his possession.

My offer was 32,000 dollars, and he said he would not sell because the prices were predicted to recover and that I should only take out student loans until the market recovered its strength. My tears were streaming down his face, and he continued to insist that he was correct and that by the time I finished college, he would have enough money to pay everything off.

I informed him that he was being a loser at the moment and that it wasn't fair that he had lied to me for such a long period of time when all he was expecting was for the stock to go back to its previous high. I should be grateful, he argued, because they only had $20,000 set aside in a shaky mutual fund, and the only reason I got $32,000 is because he made the proper investments.

Moreover, my mother is upset with me because she claims that most students do not receive financial aid from their parents while in college and that I should not be calling my father a loser for trying to give me 32,000 dollars as a gift. In fact, I'm feeling rather ungrateful and spoiled right now!

So am I the asshole?

11. THE DOWN PAYMENT

When my children went off to college, I set money aside for them to use to buy their first home when they graduated from high school. My inheritance supplied the funds for this payment.

 The only stipulation was that I had to wait a couple of years between withdrawing the funds from the account. This means that the first thing to buy was simply one house.

My eldest son and his wife were expecting a kid, so I bought their home first in 2018. Initially, my eldest was displeased, but I persuaded him that it was the better choice.

The rest of the money can now be taken out of the bank and given to my eldest child. He has now approached me with the request that I buy a home for him in the same neighbourhood as his younger sibling.

Despite this, property values nearly doubled in 2018.That is in no way covered by the funds I have set up.

So, I've caused major division in my family, with my oldest brother becoming quite enraged at me as a result of this. Please accept my apologies; nonetheless, I did not expect the market to be so prohibitively expensive. Alternatively, I promised to give him the entire sum to use as he chooses while also pledging to bequeath in my will any difference between the value of his brother's house in 2021 and the cash gift amount provided to him from my estate if the money is available.

It is because of this that we have a tense relationship with my oldest child, who took the money and moved to another state. Because of what I believed would be a nice gift, my family is now divided, which I find to be really disappointing. Because of this, the connection between my two sons has been strained even further.

Am I the Asshole?

12. MY 4 PARENTS

May is the month in which I will tie the knot with my fiancé.

Adopted as a baby, my adoptive parents (both in their 50s) did everything they could to raise me and see that I completed my education. My feelings for them are undeniable; I've always enjoyed our interactions.

The search for my biological parents began when I was 23 years old, and to cut a long storey short, they were teenagers (14 at the time of my conception). She and her husband are still married, and they have two more children. They said that they wanted to keep me but that they were unable to raise me, so they decided to place me for adoption instead. The fact that they tried to contact my adoptive parents and set up a relationship with me during my childhood and adolescence was something that really hurt me. My adoptive parents refused.

As a result, when I confronted my adoptive parents, they said that they were concerned that I might prefer my biological parents and therefore tried to keep them away from the house.

After being hurt and disappointed, I decided to use low-contact methods to communicate with others. Our relationship has improved over the years, but it isn't the same as it was previously.

I decided to have my biological father walk me down the aisle for my wedding, and he graciously accepted the invitation. My adoptive parents were disappointed and said that their worst nightmare had come true; they suggested that if I insist on putting my biological parents ahead of them, they should not be invited to the wedding.

That was my response: they aren't invited at that time. Since then, I've been referred to as an asshole by my adoptive family.

So, am I the Asshole?

13.THE INVITE

I want to preface with it is about the money and it is also not about the money. It is hurtful to be treated differently, and I know reddit believes that no one owes anyone anything, but I feel like a mom does owe her kids fair treatment.

I am getting married in May to the love of my life. I don't think my mom is a huge fan, but at least she isn't one of those crazy moms that tries to break us up. There was one incident between them, but beyond that, the relationship has been mutually civil.

I am very lucky, and my parents paid for all of my schooling, including my masters. My mom seems to think that is the norm, but I understand most parents can't do that, and I am very fortunate. My fiancée didn't have that opportunity, so she worked part time and took out loans. She currently has 80K in student loans but is working her ass off to pay them back. My dad doesn't think I should marry her while she has them, but I made it very clear that isn't up for discussion.

My dad is also paying for the wedding. When my sister got married, my dad paid for the wedding, and my mom gave her a cash gift. I don't want to get into exact numbers, but it was extremely generous and probably more than the down payment on a house. I have another sister who is getting married in September, and I found out that my mom promised her the same amount of cash but not me. I was pissed because I believed, at the time, she was doing it because she disliked my fiancée.

I confronted her and let her know if she was going to exclude my fiancée or be hurtful just because she didn't like her, there would be consequences. My mom said it wasn't about her not liking her. It was about student loans. My mom explained that both of my BILs have no debt, so the money was to start a future, but she knows if she gives me the money it will go to the loan (true), and she feels she shouldn't be responsible for someone else's kid's college education.

I tried to explain that paying down that debt ASAP is in my best interest and is in my future. My mom said that she had thought a lot about it and asked her husband for advice (they both have kids from earlier marriages and keep most of their money separate for estate planning purposes for their kids, so he doesn't have any vested interest, but he also hates me, so go figure that he said no). My mom said she feels bad, but I shouldn't punish her over a gift. I didn't say much at the time, but I thought long and hard and decided I didn't want her at the wedding.

She doesn't like my fiancée. She doesn't care about my future as much as my sisters. She is playing favourites with her kids. I texted her my decision and she never replied. My sisters now say they aren't coming to the wedding, and my father is furious and is demanding I re-invite her. My fiancée actually teared up because she feels so supported, and this does hurt, but that has to be my priority.

So, am I the Asshole?

14. CHILDFREE WEDDING

My brother is getting married this summer, and he and my future SIL recently told me they're thinking about not having any kids at their wedding.

My DS is their only nephew and will be 18 months old when they get married. I was shocked when they told me their plans. We're travelling out of state to attend, and all of our family who could watch our son will be attending the wedding. I'm in the wedding party, so I can't NOT attend and would never consider skipping my only brother's wedding anyway.

About a week later, I called my brother to tell him that I hoped they would reconsider and invite my son, and that it would mean a lot to me for him to be there to celebrate with our family. He told me that my son wouldn't remember it anyway, that their venue was really small, that they couldn't invite my kid without inviting all of their friends' kids and our cousins' kids, and that it would be more fun for me and DH to enjoy a night without our son. I reiterated that it would mean more to me for my son to be there regardless and that there is a big difference between inviting your only nephew and inviting your friends' kids. My brother and future SIL have a son a year older than mine who will be there.

My brother got really upset and complained to our parents about me. My future SIL also texted me to reiterate all my brother's points and double-down on no kids.

I have since dropped it, but it has deeply upset me that they don't want my son at their wedding. My parents are on my side (even though he has always been their favourite child), but they don't want to get involved, and I can see it starting to cause a rift. Now I'm scrambling to see if I can get childcare from a friend who happens to live a couple hours away from my brother's venue. I want to be happy for my brother, but I'm just dreading everything about this wedding now.

Should I have hidden my disappointment with their kid-free wedding decision instead of trying to talk to my brother about it? I know it's THEIR wedding and trying to get someone on the guest list who wasn't invited is an asshole move. I think that the hurt I feel, and my parents feel at my son being left out would only fester and cause long-term hard feelings regardless of whether or not I said anything.

So, am I the Asshole?

15. MORTGAGE PAYMENTS

My boyfriend (29Male) and I (22Female) recently decided to move in together. We've been together for 1.5 years. I am currently renting an apartment and he has a house that he bought just before we started dating.

Before moving in together, we thought it'd be best to discuss finances. He's a doctor, and I'm a social media manager. He told me how much he makes, and it was more or less what I expected. When I told him how much I make, he kind of laughed and said I should tell him how much I make per month, not per year. I told him no, that's how much I make per month. His shock was understandable to me; I make 150% of his salary.

I told him that it's just because I work for a client in a country where the currency is nearly 20x stronger. If I had this same job in our country, I would only make a quarter of what he makes.

I don't live an extravagant lifestyle, so you wouldn't be able to tell that I make as much money as I do by just looking at me. I still live in a small apartment that I got when I was making less than 20% of what I make now, and I never learned how to drive (I know, I know), so I don't have a car and get around exclusively by e-hailing services.

Once the first shock wore off, he said, "That's great, because now I can pay half of his mortgage."

I was a little taken aback by that. I mean, it's not like I wasn't going to contribute to the household at all. I would've been happy to buy groceries, pay utilities, cook, and clean because my workload is MUCH lighter than his. I told him this and that I wouldn't pay half his mortgage.

He retorted that since I make so much more than him, the least I could do is pay just half the mortgage and that we could spend half on groceries and utilities.

I told him that that's a little unfair because if we break up, he gets a house and I'm left with nothing, and that if that's going to be the case, I will rather stay in my apartment.

I offered up a compromise. His house is sparsely decorated, to say the least. He has 2x1-seat couches, a table that's too big and a TV that's too small. Oh, and a bed. He's never really there, so I get it. I told him that I would give the entire house, get the groceries, cook and clean, and we'd split the cost of utilities. But he still insisted that I pay half of the mortgage.

He said that I still need a place to live, and that if I was going to be paying rent anyway, paying his mortgage would be the same thing. He said I was being an A-hole for not wanting to pay it.

My boyfriend is a smart man, so I don't know if he doesn't see the logic (or lack thereof, in my opinion) of what he's saying or if I'm being dumb and it's not a big deal.

So, am I the Asshole?

16. THE DRESSING

So, last night me and a few friends went to a pizza shop in downtown Morgantown. We got a couple of pizzas, some regular and some gourmet. We didn't know, but every pizza came with a cup of garlic sauce. Well, none of us liked garlic sauce, so we asked if we could get some ranch instead. They wanted a dollar per cup and wouldn't swap the garlic sauce. Keep in mind, these were large pizzas and very hungry college students, and we would have needed about 10 of these little cups of ranch.

We weren't about to pay $10 for ranch dressing and told the girl who brought out the pizza not to worry about the ranch. The restaurant owner overheard this and made a comment, "shit isn't free, boys," and that really pissed me off. There was a convenience store across the street, and I decided to get us some ranch. I got up and walked across the street and bought a big bottle of ranch, good for five more pizza outings for $5.

Some of my friends said I shouldn't have done that, and the store owner gave me a dirty look. I was told I was "petty" and "tight". I told them I was going to enjoy my cheap ranch and if it was that big of a personal conviction, to keep their hands off it. That personal conviction lasted 30 seconds, and pretty soon that bottle was being passed around the table.

Remember, they gave out the garlic sauce and refused to substitute ranch. It was frustrating and strange, to say the least.

I'm the asshole for refusing to pay $10 for ranch and instead going to buy my own bottle.

JAMIE GOLDSON

So Am I the Asshole

17. THE PLANE TICKETS

I'm going to be really quick here.

My brother's wedding is days away. My wife stated she didn't want to go because she wanted to stay home with the kids (she is a stay at home mother while I'm the breadwinner, as they call it). I tried to convince her to go, but to no avail. She wanted to sit this one out, and I respected her wishes.

I booked a first-class ticket and am currently packing since the trip takes five days. My wife last night told me she had changed her mind and wanted to go with me to the wedding. I said great, but the argument started when she expected me to book her a first class ticket on the same plane I was on. I said it was impossible since reservations had been made ahead of time and there was no empty spot in the first class. She said fine and would catch the next plane, but I had to book her in first class as well, to which I said no, because I had already set a budget for her, but since she said she wasn't going, I spent the money on stuff I needed for the trip. She asked what she was going to do then, and I suggested that she pay for her own first class tickets. She didn't take it well and called me a asshole for suggesting that since, unlike me, she has no money and since she takes care of the house and kids, I should be paying for her ticket as an appreciative gesture and added that I probably didn't want her to go and was making excuses by refusing to pay for tickets to get her to stay home with the kids. I told her it wasn't my fault. She said she wasn't going and ended up spending the money I set aside for the tickets. She said I still have money and can afford a ticket for her, and as her husband and breadwinner, that's my obligation, but I refused and told her she needed to figure out these arrangements on her own since she changed her mind at the last minute. She got upset and said I was awful and selfish for thinking it was OK to leave her behind like that. I insisted it was her fault from the beginning for not being straightforward, but she keeps saying I'm selfish and want to exclude her from her brother-in-law's wedding.

She has been arguing with me about it since last night and is making me feel awful with the names she is calling me after she said she won't forgive me for causing her to miss the wedding.

So, am I the Asshole?

18. WORKING WITH MY SISTER?

My sister started a company last year. I was feeling stifled in my last career path, and I wanted to do something different. I jumped in with my sister. It meant a massive pay cut and an increase in responsibility. We can live comfortably off his income, so we didn't change our lifestyle at all.

I am learning new things every day. I love working with my sister. She is smart and talented. There is always a new challenge that we have to solve. I am doing things that I never imagined I could. The hours are longer, but I love every second of it.

We were supposed to go out last week, but I had to cancel because we had an issue with a vendor that needed to be dealt with. I apologized, but he was very upset about it. I have had to prioritise the business a few times before, but he has always been understanding. I usually get back home after he has gone to bed, but he was waiting for me that day. He was stewing and he was really angry. He said I was being an errand girl for my sister, and I should realise my own value. He said my job was an absolutely shit deal for our family as I was gone longer, and we made less money.

He said he wanted me to quit my job and find something that paid better. I told him that I wouldn't be quitting. I loved what I did, and I hated that he was undermining my work. He just stopped arguing with me and said we could talk about it later. I feel like an asshole because this is literally the first time my husband has been this angry and bitter. I have never seen him this upset. He is being very withdrawn, and he is purposely working longer hours, so we don't really see each other. I feel like I fucked up here. My husband is upset and hurt, and I don't want to quit at all.

So am I the asshole?

19. I JUST WANT WHAT'S BEST FOR US

My boyfriend and I have been dating for a year, and it's been mostly good. Except he doesn't make much and I have to pay for everything not related to basic necessities. We don't leave together at the moment, so he pays for his rent, car, and food, and that's about all he can afford. Whenever we go out, I have to pay for all the date nights, trips, and even gas for road trips since he can't afford anything but the basics. He makes $28,000 as a meat packer, and I make $94,000 as a data engineer. I don't care that he makes less, but he makes so little that in our area he can't afford much besides going to work and going to sleep. If we want to go camping, I have to buy or rent all the equipment, pay for gas, pay for the park fees and camping site, etc. Otherwise, we can only sit at home and play video games or cook something together, which we do, but I don't want to do that every weekend.

The other problem is that he doesn't have much motivation to get skills or get a better job. He worked for the meatpackers after finishing a semester at culinary school, but he only did that because his dad is a chef. I don't think he is depressed or anything like that. I've known him since high school and he's always kind of been this way. After high school, I went to college and dated guys while working. They made more and had more motivation, but they were flaky and just wanted someone to sleep with. He is actually someone who wants a family, but now I'm worried about how we can be compatible in marriage when he isn't motivated to better himself. Also, I don't want to carry him financially through the marriage.

My friend has an auto body shop, and he likes to hang out there. I've been searching for mechanic courses and sent them to him, asking him if he was interested. He got mad at me, saying I was judging him for not having a fancy job, but he was happy with his current job. He just goes there and goes home, and he doesn't want to go to school or put anything more into what he just considers a means of survival. We had a fight in which I told him that I was finding it difficult to see a future for us when I had to pay for everything in the relationship. He told me I was just going to have to accept him or leave and stormed out.

So am I the asshole?

20. THE HISTORICAL SOCIETY

My parents were really pushing me (16m) to get a summer job this year. I chose not to, instead deciding to volunteer at our town's historical society. It's super close, so I can literally walk there. I really enjoy working there because I'm always learning new things about our town and about preserving historical materials, and because I enjoy talking with the people who do come in. It's also gotten me interested in becoming an archivist. My history teacher will volunteer too, so it's nice to get to see a different side of him than I usually do in class.

Unfortunately for me, my parents have a rule that says if I want to buy anything over the summer, I need to make the money myself. For whatever reason, this also means that I also have to pay them a small fee once a week to even just use the television, which I haven't been able to pay for over a month. This rule has been there since my older brother (20m) got his first job at 15. Since my sister (16f) has a job, she has money to do what she wants, even though I spend way more hours a week working than she does. My parents have said that they would give me an allowance if I did an internship or something like that, yet they won't consider giving me an allowance for what I'm doing now.

At dinner, I got into an argument with my parents after I suggested that they give me an allowance. They told me that volunteering at the historical society isn't something that warrants one, and that I should stop being lazy and either get an internship somewhere or get a job. I told them that it was unfair that even though I work more than my sister does, they wouldn't even let me watch television. They explained to me that working at the historical society doesn't teach skills that will be valuable to me in the future and called it a glorified hobby. I told them that what they said was a load of crap, and then they started yelling at me.

So, am I the Asshole?

21. MY COUSIN JOSH

My cousin, Josh, and I were roommates. We were all close and had gone to college together. My cousin started seeing this guy soon after we moved in. He was rude and he always left a mess, but these were minor problems. Everyone adjusted to it, but things started going south when he realised that Josh was gay. He was weird and made some crass "jokes" about it. Josh had always been a shy guy, and he just retreated back into his room when her boyfriend was around.

I talked to her about him. She defended him and told me to not take things he said too seriously. I stopped hanging out with her and spent more time with Josh and my other friends. She moved out at the end of the lease, and I've had only limited contact with her ever since. They got married, and I went to their wedding. This was a few years ago.

Last month, I was looped into a conversation about filling an open position that would work closely with me and a few other people working under me. The two people being talked about were her husband and another candidate, but they liked her husband more due to the fact that he was related to a client and his resume did look a bit better.

I told them that I had interacted with him and recounted my interactions with him, taking time to highlight his homophobia as we have a few LGBT employees. My opinion swung the decision towards the other candidate.

I didn't think much of it until last week when my brother was talking about how badly my cousin was doing financially and I told him that her husband had applied for a role, but I told them that he was a bad fit. I told this to my brother in confidence.

He told our parents, and they are not very pleased. He has repeatedly told me to move on from our fights as roommates and that they are disappointed in me for not helping my family.

From what I heard from my brother, they are in a bad spot and this job was a really good one, and my actions cost him the job. I don't like my cousin, but I don't want her to suffer, and I feel some guilt about that.

So, am I the Asshole?

22. THE TEACHER

I'm a middle school teacher, teaching beginners a foreign language. My students are just starting out, learning to count, the alphabet, introductions, etc. I have a student this year whose mother had already taught him this language. This poses a problem, specifically because it completely ruins the classroom setup.

This student finishes his work very quickly and then starts getting bored and distracting others. I tell him to work more slowly and conscientiously, but it doesn't really work, so he ends up either doodling or doing homework from other classes during this time.

I recently had a meeting with his mother, who was unhappy with the way I was teaching her son. I told her that unfortunately it isn't my job to teach high-level students and there was nothing I could do for him besides request he sit out (there is no higher-level language class as it's just an option in their last year here).

The mother was disappointed and said she specifically chose this school because we offer this language and said she would talk to the principal about it. My principal is incredibly strict and has no understanding of teachers' having free time, so I suspect he will try to enforce me teaching this student extra things during class, which frankly, I don't have time for. My job is to teach everyone, not just one person. But when I was venting to the other teachers, they said my attitude towards the mother was assholish and that it "wouldn't be that hard" to set up something else for this kid. I respectfully disagreed, but now I'm wondering if I'm wrong.

So, am I the asshole?

23. SHE JUST NEEDS TO DO HER JOB

 I have about 14 colleagues and a boss. Of the 16 of us, only 3 of us do not have children. I am one of the ones that does. I have three of them. I'm also a single mom.

The issue: One of my co-workers with a kid definitely plays the mom card. I usually hate using that term as shit comes up when you have kids. But she uses this as an excuse for why she can never come in on time, why she needs to leave early, why she's always so preoccupied with her phone, why she can't focus on what she's doing, so she screws up and we have to fix her mistakes, etc. Her kid is 9 years old and in school all day (not even doing virtual learning, but in school). He's a neurotypical kid with no health issues. I get worried about him, but like I said, about 80% of us have kids. We all still show up and do our job. And honestly, the excuse of "I have a kid" wears thin, especially about coming in early and late because her husband doesn't work, so he can take care of their son. Our boss defends her and refuses to do anything about her negligence. I do blame our boss more, because she just allowed it to happen. But I do think my co-worker needs to step up while we're at work. I have tried talking to her nicely. She says she'll do better and never does. I've asked if she needs help with something, offering support, and she says she's fine. I also went to HR, and they didn't do anything except hold a meeting and tell us all that we needed to pull our weight. Nothing changed.

The other day, she screwed up again. She was on her phone, like she is most of the day, and wasn't giving it her all. It was a huge mistake that nearly cost us a client, and it's one that she's made several times before. I admit, I wasn't nice to her about this. I didn't yell, but my tone was clipped, and I told her that she needed to put the damn phone away and actually pay attention to what she was doing. She got in a tizzy, saying that she was texting her husband about their son, and she didn't mean to, she was sorry, etc. I said it wasn't okay and she needed to just focus. She then tried saying, "I have a kid, my mind is in two places." I told her, "I have three kids that all go to different schools." I am here every morning on time. I stay until it's time to go. I may have to take a call for my kids occasionally. I get you think about kids all the time, but I also manage to do my job. This excuse just doesn't fly anymore. Do your damn job. " She quickly went about fixing her mistake, and I walked away.

She didn't go to HR or our boss over it, but someone else who overheard it did. I was severely reprimanded for this, saying that it's not my job to have that talk with her. I said maybe not, but the people whose job it was weren't doing anything. I didn't get a formal write-up, but things are tense.

Some of my co-workers think I did the right thing; others think I should've documented it with HR and let it go. I'm torn.

So, am I the Asshole?

24. MY DAUGHTER THE BULLY

I have three children who I share custody of.

My youngest daughter has graduated from high school. But we found out that for the 6 months prior, she and her friends had been bullying my stepdaughter at school.

After getting more info from my stepdaughter's friend, it appears that my daughter's friends instigated the bullying, while my daughter would often laugh at her stepsister's expense. I think this made her just as culpable as her friends. Even if my daughter claims that she can't control what other people say about her stepsister,

So, the consequence of this was to cancel the graduation party I normally throw for my children who graduated.

In the past, I had an aunt who gave each child a $40,000 check to use for their college. It's been a huge help because my ex and I aren't well off. She gave these checks at the graduation parties.

For my daughter, my aunt asked when we'd have the party so she could give the cheque. As a consequence, I told her we weren't planning a party. She understood and said she'd bring the cheque when we met up in the future.

Unfortunately, my aunt passed away a month after what should've been the party date. We had never gotten to meet her before then.

And her children are denying the existence of any cheque for my daughter, which may well be the case.

This has created a huge conflict between my daughter and myself.

She had been counting on the money to live on her own closer to campus and take out significantly fewer loans.

But now, she's going to have to live at home and take out loans. I've co-signed these loans for her because I feel terrible about it. I've tried talking to her about it and how I wish it hadn't gone this way, but she's completely iced all of us out.

She moved down into our basement and doesn't come up anymore. She hasn't talked to me, my wife, or my stepdaughter since.

I do feel very badly that she lost out on the gift, and I feel very guilty about it. But I truly believed that I was delivering a proper punishment at the time.

So, am I the Asshole?

25. MY EX-WIFE'S WEIGHT LOSS

Shortly before my divorce in early 2020, my ex-wife had weight loss surgery. To clarify, I don't think that there's anything wrong with having that type of surgery if needed. I'm a chubby guy myself, and I've struggled with my weight at different times throughout my life. We had a pretty rough divorce, but I don't hate her or anything. However, I feel it's safe to say that we don't have the best relationship if you would even consider us having one at all.

I haven't spoken to her in 20 months, and the next thing I know, I'm getting long strings of angry Facebook Messenger texts about how it's not my place to tell her business, etc.

This is what happened a few weeks prior to this. One of my co-workers (a mutual acquaintance) mentioned that they saw her the other day and remarked about how much weight she had lost. I said something really quickly, like, "Oh cool, the surgery must have worked well," and then I didn't really think much about it.

I've never really thought that weight loss surgery was weird or a taboo topic to talk about, or something to be embarrassed about. After getting chewed out, I checked her Facebook out of curiosity, and I noticed that on any picture where she posted about her weight loss, there would be multiple people asking her what her "secret" was, and "how did you do it?" and she would flat out ignore those comments.

I get that perhaps she's self-conscious about it, but I'm stuck between "I'm not a mind-reader, and I can't possibly know one person's every insecurity" and "Maybe this is some taboo topic that I wasn't aware of, and I was being an asshole without realising it."

60

So, am I the asshole?

26. THE WEDDING PHOTOS

I (27Female) recently got married to my partner (29Male) of 8 years. We had a very small ceremony and reception on the east coast, which is where I've lived for 9 years and where my husband's family is located. I am from the west coast, so the bulk of my extended family and friends couldn't attend. We only invited our immediate family and friends so as to not pressure my whole family to book flights for my wedding.

One of my bridesmaids, Elle (24Female), was visibly pregnant during the ceremony (19 weeks). I have known Elle literally my entire life; my SAHM was best friends with her mom and provided free day-care for her and her 2 sisters. I honestly think of her as my own sister.

Less than two weeks after the wedding, Elle miscarried. My husband and I were on our honeymoon, so she waited to tell us until we returned, about a week after it happened. I was devastated for her. I flew to the west coast the moment I heard and spent a few days taking care of Elle, her husband, and her home while they grieved. This was about a week ago.

Here's where my problem begins. I recently received my wedding photos from my photographer. We paid extra to have the photos prioritised so I could show my family who couldn't attend the wedding right away. I told Elle that the photos were ready, and she at once called me to ask that I not share the photos yet. She said she wasn't ready to see anything that reminded her of her pregnancy and that the miscarriage wasn't public information yet. I said I understood and asked when she thought she would be ready. She didn't know.

My solution was to make a private Facebook group where I posted only photos from the wedding that didn't show Elle. I did, however, send all of the pictures privately over email to my grandmother, who wasn't well enough to fly to the wedding due to a years-long battle with cancer. My grandmother (who thinks of Elle as one of her own grandchildren) at once emailed her to tell her how beautiful she looked and how she couldn't "wait to help welcome the child" and many other things about motherhood. Additionally, she shared some photos with more people who contacted Elle.

Elle blew up at me, screaming that I didn't care about her, talking about how insensitive I was for sending photos of my honeymoon to her while she was grieving (before she told me), and went so far as to blame "the stress of the wedding" for "killing her baby." I paid for her flights, accommodations, and dress, and planned everything. All she had to do was be present for the 5 days surrounding my wedding. Perhaps most importantly, she was upset with me for sharing the photos against her will, before she was ready. I've just been giving her space since then, so we haven't spoken.

I wish I could take back what happened, but I can't tell if what I did was really an asshole move or if this is grief talking.

So am I the Asshole?

27. THE LOST TOY

A few months ago, it was my daughter's 5th birthday. My sister-in-law (42f) barely keeps in touch with our kids despite living in the same town and comes out of the woodwork twice a year to give them a birthday and Christmas present. All my in-laws aren't particularly close to one another—not through any estrangement, they are just not very close. I tend not to push the issue as my kids have lots of loving aunties and uncles on my side of the family that they see all the time.

Anyway, my sister-in-law gets my daughter a golliwog doll. I'm horrified, but don't say anything at the time. She says she saw it and it reminded her of a doll she had when she was a kid and that she loved it. My daughter is delighted.

Later that night, I asked my husband if he understood the context of golliwogs as a racist caricature of a minstrel and if his sister knew that too. He says he knows what they represented decades ago but that our 5-year-old daughter doesn't, and if she likes the doll, what's the harm? (Also, we are white and live in Australia, which does have its own history of racism, but obviously not America's history). I'm pissed off and making my feelings known about how offensive these dolls are, and that his sister should know better too, since she's an educated woman. (She is the CFO).

I decided to just get rid of the doll. I wait a few weeks and see that my daughter isn't particularly attached to it; it mostly just sits on her bed with the rest of her stuffed toys. I test the idea of throwing it away first--I hide it for a few days to see if she notices. She doesn't, so into the bin it goes.

They scheduled a zoom call a few nights ago. On the call, my SIL asks my daughter how she is enjoying the doll. The daughter goes to find it and realises it's missing and is distraught. Her distress carries on for some time after the call, and she keeps apologising to me for not looking after her toys. I comfort her and say that it's OK, but don't tell her the truth.

Later that evening, my husband confronts me and asks if I threw it away. I admit it, and he gets angry, saying that if that was my plan, I should have told my daughter the truth and explained why the doll couldn't be in our house, so she knew that it wasn't her fault the doll was missing.

I think a 5-year-old is too young to understand and would see me throwing away her doll as a punishment for no reason. I do think it's important to educate our kids on racism, but only when it's age-appropriate. I just don't think my daughter would have been able to separate throwing away a toy from a valuable lesson on racism.

So, am I the Asshole?

28. MY DAUGHTER THE THIEF

My daughter Sarah has been getting worse and worse lately. A few years ago, she was perfect. She was happy and bubbly and did really well at school. Like many girls her age, she loved her hair and clothes and fashion. She was and still is all pink and girly. Since she was little, she's wanted to be a doctor, something we've strongly encouraged but without putting any pressure on her.

Unfortunately, she met a new group of friends last year, and since then her behaviour has gotten much worse. She's started speaking in a fake "street" accent and talking in slang words which we don't even understand half of. We live in a nice area, and her friends are all fairly well-off, but they're all into this style too.

Academically, she's still doing very well. Behaviour-wise, that isn't the case. She's sworn at teachers and been accused of bullying other kids. My wife and I have been called in on numerous occasions.

I was going to work today when I went to the shop to get a bottle of water. I've known the guy who works there for years, and he told me that he'd had to ban my daughter from the shop, as she'd tried to steal several items.

When I got home, I sat Sarah down, told her what the shop guy told me, and said I had called the police and they were on their way. She at once got scared, asking what would happen to her. I said anything could happen, and I decided to scare her by saying she may even be sent to prison. She burst into tears and was sobbing and begging me to call the police off.

In the end, I felt bad about seeing her so upset and told her there were no police coming, but that she needed to behave better or there would be next time. She ran upstairs in tears, didn't come down, and cried herself to sleep.

My wife was really angry with me, saying it was cruel of me to scare her like that. I said it was a final warning for if she does anything like that again. I WILL call the police if I find out she's been stealing again.

I've never seen Sarah so upset, and it was a shame to see her like that, but we didn't raise her to be a thief or a bully, so she should expect consequences.

So, am I the asshole?

29. THE 30-YEAR DECEPTION

I (30 f) have always been a family history buff, so naturally I did an ancestry test years ago. I connected with some distant cousins and had some connections I couldn't place but didn't think too much about it. Anyhow, 7 years later, a half-sister contacts me, informing me I'm her half-sister. which is impossible. I'm an IVF baby and have always been told stories about it being the last round, etc. Now I'm thinking there's been a mix up at the hospital and my parents will be devastated. Then I realise my actual sister is also only coming up as a half-sister, but I'd never thought much about it.

I called the hospital, who didn't even have a record of my mum but suggested I was a donor baby and my parents lied. I'm in denial. It's impossible!

I got up the courage to message mum. She's cagey. I'll organise a call. She makes me reveal that I knew it before she admits it.

I tell them I still love them the same and not to feel guilty, but that I'm really upset, and it will take me time to come to terms with it. I feel like I've been really mature about what is a soul-crushing revelation for me. Not only did my parents lie to me for 30 years, I missed out on my siblings' lives, and I feel absolutely gross about how I was conceived. I don't know who I am anymore, and I feel disgusted. I may never find all of my siblings, but there are at least 10 families with my siblings out there.

I asked my mom for information to find the donor and to get the medical history. She refused and told me that she was sad too, and I felt she made it all about her. She told me I'd put her through things too and she got over it, and how could I expect her to reveal this to a moody teenager? Well, I'm 30 now. You'd have thought finding out I took the ancestry test when I was 23 would have been a perfect time instead of waiting for an internet stranger.

I asked my parents to go to therapy, and they refused. I told them I just wanted an apology for lying for 30 years and for them to admit and own the wrong call. I want them to take responsibility for their choices and how they affect me. Does that make me the AH? I'm trying to be a grown up about it, but the responses from my parents are alienating me and making me want to cut contact. I sent dad a nice message after that, and he only sent 2 words back. It's been 3 days and neither of them has called me to check on me. I'm having a mental breakdown.

So, am I the asshole?

30. MY HUSBAND'S FAVOURITE CHILD

When I met my husband, he had a fifteen-year-old daughter, who was, for the most part, easy to get along with, though ridiculously spoiled. His daughter's mother had some mental issues, and he was a single dad for most of her childhood. He said he never wanted kids and that she had been a result of birth control failure and that he didn't want anymore.

I told him that not having kids was a dealbreaker for me, and he quickly reconsidered. His daughter was seventeen when our daughter was born, and I was shocked at how jealous she was. In general, she is not the clingy emotional type, but she was furious. He made it his priority to make her feel better and reassure her that she was always going to be the important one. My stepdaughter went to college and thrived, and we had another child. She wasn't even jealous at that time, but he still made a big production of loving her more.

Right now, our kids are 13 and 15 and my stepdaughter is 32, married with kids, and living on her own, but it is still pretty clear that he favours her. They talk on the phone almost daily, but he has a hard time talking to our daughters because they are "too emotional."

Right now, he is visiting his oldest daughter at her beach house, and we weren't invited because she hates our 13-year-old. My daughter did go through a phase of being very rude and acting out, but we did therapy and discipline, and it is under control right now. I told him he shouldn't go see his daughter because it is rude to exclude his wife and kids, and he said he doesn't care if she is rude, she's still his daughter.

In the past, when the kids said something, I made excuses for him. We Face Timed today and my 13-year old made a comment about my stepdaughter being his favourite, and I just said, "I'm sorry honey." When the kids got off the phone, he got mad at me for not correcting her, but I said I'm not going to lie about it anymore. He has admitted to me in private that she is his favourite, but he says it's not his fault and he can't control how he feels.

So, am I the asshole?

31. MY SON'S GRANDMA

I have two kids, a 9-year-old son and a 7-year-old daughter. My son is technically my stepson, though. When I married my husband, he had a 1-year-old baby and I adopted him. My son's biological mother has never been in the picture. We are very open about this with him. We have told him that I used to be his stepmom before I adopted him and have answered any questions that he has about it.

My mother has always seemed to prefer my daughter over my son due to the fact that she is my biological child. Both of my children received Christmas cards from my mom. Gabrielle (my daughter) had $20 inside of her card. My son didn't have any money in his. Logan (my son) asked me why there was no money on his card, and I didn't know how to explain it to him. So, I took my own $20 and pretended to pick it up off of the floor. I told him that he must have dropped his money on the floor.

My children are using Facetime to communicate with my mother. My son said, "Thank you for the card and the $20, Grandma." And my mother basically told him that she gave $20 to Gabrielle because she could only afford to give biological grandchildren money. Logan was very confused and kept insisting that there was money in his card. So, I basically had to end up telling the truth that I had pretended to give him $20, and that the money was actually from me.

Now my child is upset at me because I lied to him. And he is very upset in general because he knows that his grandma thinks less of him because he is not my biological child. I also think he is very confused about why she thinks less of him. I probably shouldn't have lied to him, but I didn't know what else to do. "Grandma didn't give you money because you aren't my biological child," I can tell my child. I have always raised them both equally, despite his not being biological. His not getting any money makes it seem like he is not as important as his sister. But that is not true in the slightest. He is just as important as she is.

So am I the Asshole?

32. THE MAID OF DISHONOUR

I have two friends, Daisy and Marie. They went to high school together as well. Daisy was the most popular girl in school, and she was also very mean-girlish. I knew she had some history with Marie, but neither had shared many details. Daisy has told me some things about her life when she was younger, and it was a mess. She was out of control. Her mom is the worst, and her dad had like 4 or 5 wives.

Daisy and I are friends due to her and her husband's spending summers in my state. Marie lives here, but usually spends most of the summer in the cape, so they haven't had to mingle too much, outside of a couple parties at my house. We are all in our early thirties now, so high school was roughly 13 years ago.

When I got engaged, I asked Daisy to be a bridesmaid and Marie to be the MOH and they both accepted. Daisy was down here for Thanksgiving, and we did a lot of wedding planning. Marie was very quiet every time Daisy was around. Daisy then invited me on a trip for her birthday and casually invited Marie because she felt bad that her husband was out of the country on business (Daisy is super co-dependent with her husband and if he is out of town she makes her sister sleep with her, so I think this was genuine). Marie ended up going because she is bad at saying no, but she broke down crying at the hotel because she is still afraid of Daisy and shared with me some of the things Daisy did to her in high school and how they still affect her life today and she struggles a lot with self-esteem.

It did change the way I saw Daisy a little. When we got back to our state, I asked Marie how she felt about Daisy being a bridesmaid, and she said it was giving her anxiety and bringing up bad feelings, and it is hard to see how happy Daisy is because Marie's mom gave her the cliche speech about how Daisy was going to peak in high school. I decided I didn't want Marie to feel this way and asked Daisy to step back as a bridesmaid.

Daisy got very upset and said she had been nothing but nice to Marie through this and they were both kids. I said I still want her at the wedding, but I think this is too hard on Marie, especially with the destination bachelorette party and she would have to be in close quarters with Daisy for multiple days. Daisy said she won't be at the wedding and hasn't been talking to me. Daisy's husband sent me a long message about how I am ridiculous for punishing her for stuff she did as a kid, and haven't I evolved from the time I was a teenager. He said knowing what I know about how dysfunctional her home life was, I should have more empathy. Daisy's husband actually knew her in high school and hated her, so I get what he is saying. I feel a little bad because it was a long time ago, but at the same time I feel like if one person has to be uncomfortable it should be Daisy, the person who started this.

So, am I the asshole?

33. THE MEAN GIRLS' MUM

So, I work at a department store in a mall near where I grew up. I was bullied in HS. It wasn't to the end of my rope, but it wasn't pleasant. I don't think about it a lot, but sometimes people from HS come through my store. I just do my job and am pleasant to them because I need the money.

Anyway, a woman came through to pick up an order, and she gave me the last name and spelled it. I thought, "Hey, that's Kristin and Katie's last names from HS." It was a pretty unique one.

At first, I didn't say anything, just normal, pleasant chatter. She took the stuff out of the bag to make sure it was right and commented, "My daughters will love these. They just finished college," etc., etc. She essentially confirmed whose mom she was.

I was just making small talk and said, "Oh, I think I went to school with a Kristin and Katie Lastname."

She said, "Oh yeah?! How funny! Were you friends? "

I said, "Oh no, I just knew they were in my grade."

She said, "Were you on the volleyball team with them?"

I said, "No, I don't think so."

She looked at my nametag and said, "That's odd. I think I remember them talking about a penny back then!" You must've come over for their birthday or something.

That just kind of made me sad, because I've never been to a birthday party before, and I said, "No, I definitely never came over. Kristin bullied me, and I don't think I ever talked to Katie. "

Her entire demeanour changed (which was okay, honestly, I had people in line). She didn't say a single thing after that and just kind of left without taking her order sheet. I didn't chase her down to get it to her. She'll have a copy in her email anyway.

The next customer in line said something like, "That was awkward!" and my co-worker at the counter agreed. They both laughed about it, but later on, my co-worker said that it was pretty douchey to tell a parent that their kid was a bully. She has a daughter. I don't have kids. I have a betta fish named Karl.

On the one hand, yeah, I guess. It was like 4 years ago. But at the same time, it happened, and I'd think a parent would WANT to know that their kid was a asshole to others so they could talk about it. Even as adults. SO am I the Asshole?

34. THE (EX) FRIENDS

This just happened a few weeks ago, but I graduated from high school in 1988.

My wife and I were out for dinner and drinks and met up with some friends. We bumped into an older friend, Dan, from high school and his wife and friends. Basically, everyone knew everyone else.

As the night went on, we talked about who we still keep in contact with. In high school, I hung with a couple of friend groups and am still close to one of them. The other friend group consisted of Dan and another kid named Mike.

After we graduated, I basically stopped talking to both of them. Dan assumed that I drifted away from the other friend group as well. He was a bit shocked that I was still in contact with them. Just an FYI, with the exception of LinkedIn I do not have a social media presence.

He just assumed we drifted apart after college. He asked what happened.

Here is where I might be an asshole because of how truthful I was.

My father passed away in my senior year in March. Mind you, Dan and Mike were over at my house a lot and knew my dad. They were fascinated with war-related stuff, and my dad served in Korea and was highly decorated.

When he passed, they never called, and they didn't show up at the wake or funeral. I took a week off after his funeral, and when

I saw them again, I got what I thought was a half-assed "sorry, how are you doing". Nothing like your mom or anything. Meanwhile, my friends Sean and Chris were by my side the whole time. That pissed me off, and I realised they were shitty friends and shitty people. That and a few other choice comments too. So, I told him all of this.

Well, he got uncomfortable and tried to mumble an apology, and I told him it was not important and not to bother. It kind of killed the mood for the rest of the night and everyone left shortly thereafter.

My wife said I didn't have to be so detailed in my response back to Dan, and while it was amusing to see the look on his face, I was an asshole for being blunt and ruining the night.

So am I the asshole?

35. MY SON'S SALARY

My son [17], husband and I have had an arrangement with my son since he got his first job at the local fast food restaurant at age 15. To help prepare him for university or his first job, we agreed to set up a separate long-term savings account in which a certain percentage of his final pay each week would go into this account.

At age 15, 50% of his wage would go into this savings account, and the other 50% he could keep in his own everyday account to do as he pleased. As he aged a year, we reduced the ratio of savings to his own account, i.e., at 16, it was 60-40: 40% in the savings account and 60% of his own money. At 17, it's 70-30 (30% going into his savings account). This was done with the intention that as he got older, he would become more responsible for his own income and probably want to buy more "big name" things like computers, phones, and possibly a car. But he would still have savings there for graduation. When he turns 18, his income will be entirely his own. We will give him the account number for the savings account, and it will be his choice to put in as much or as little, if at all, of his wage. He won't be able to access this savings account until he graduates.

My son was happy with this arrangement, until now. He came home from school upset and angry about his wages being "stolen". Apparently, his friends at school think it's stupid that I take "half" his money (like I said, it's not half, it's 30%, the remaining 70% is his to do whatever the heck he wants with it). Even a couple of his friend's parents find it a little strange that I would take my son's money. My son now wants complete ownership of his money that he earns and also wants early access to the savings account because it's his money too and I "have no right to steal it from him."

I told him that while I understand his frustration, I also believe that setting up good saving habits now will help him in the future, and when he sees how much money has been put away in this account for him over the years, he will see the hard work pay off. I also reminded him that when he turns 18, we respect his position as a new adult, and he will be able to do what he likes with 100% of his wages. He said he got that, but now he wants it all in, which I flat out refused again, citing my reasons. This caused a huge argument, which ended with me sending him to his room without his phone for the night and taking away his Xbox for the week.

I spoke to my sister, and while she agrees with my intentions, she believes I should also respect that this is indeed my son's money, and if he now wants all of it, we should allow that. My husband still agrees to keep the savings account closed until our son graduates but is now leaning towards letting him keep all his income. I still believe in the 70-30 split. I believe when he sees the savings account, he will be a lot more appreciative, and when he is 18, next year will be entirely his own. SO am I the Asshole for wanting to keep the income split?

So am I the asshole

36.THE BREAKFAST THIEF

I have been with my girlfriend for 7 months. We don't live together, and she has sleep-overs at my place regularly.

Two days ago, she spent the night at my place, and in the morning, while I was sleeping, she got up, got dressed, took my credit card, and went grocery shopping with it. I woke up to a massive breakfast made by her as a surprise, and when I asked how she got money and time to prepare all that, she told me she took my credit card while I was sleeping and headed to the super-market to get the stuff, she needed to make me a surprise breakfast. I was stunned. I asked why she didn't ask before taking my credit card and she said I was sleeping, and she didn't want to bother me. Besides that, she wanted this to be a surprise. I just stared and said, "I don't know, you do realise you technically stole from me when you took my credit card and went shopping with it without my consent, right?". She looked at me in complete shock and confusion and said that she was just trying to do something nice for me, and I just implied that she was a thief. I just shrugged and said it was technically true. She was so upset that she got up and stormed out of the kitchen crying. She collected her stuff and left after she said she spent time and effort preparing me breakfast, and I was out of line to say she stole from me just because she forgot her wallet at home. She kept hanging up when I tried calling her, and later sent me money for the stuff she bought, although she didn't take anything with her.

My sister came over and when I told her, she called me an ungrateful asshole with no manners to react this way after this display of affection by my girlfriend. She suggested I get over myself and apologise as soon as possible, but I decided to take my time.

So, am I the asshole?

37. THE PRANK

I bought a house seven years ago, and I met my fiancé, Al, four years ago. This year, he moved in. We're talking about making it a home for both of us.

But as of now, he hasn't moved much stuff in. Right now, 95% of the stuff and furniture in the house is mine.

When his mom comes over, she's kind of a snoop. He was used to that, but when she comes to our house, it's so uncomfortable because she's just going through my shit.

When I am bothered, she's like, "I was just helping with chores" etc. He says I should just let her because she has "a lot of nervous energy."

One thing she snooped on was actually embarrassing. In my home office, I had a little "affirmation" post-it note on my monitor saying "I am smart, I am skilled, I am deserving of great things." It was a silly thing, but my therapist recommended it to get me in a confident mindset before an interview.

Anyway, she made a comment about my ego...

But as a joke, I decided to do it again. I had my best friend over, and we got drunk on wine and wrote a bunch of "affirmations" to hide.

Some were:

My teeth will grow back! I am sharklike and powerful!

Kitchen drawers: I know when to spoon, but I also know when to fork! I am sexy and self-assured!

Work Desk: I will not just fuck my way to the top of the company, I will fuck my way to the top of the world!

I walk into a closet: I am beautiful both with and without clothes! Especially without! My boobs are legendary!

There were a bunch more, and my friend and I had a hilarious time writing them.

Next time my Mother in law came over, she saw a few. And she didn't acknowledge them to me, despite the fact that she had begun acting strangely towards me.

I went to run some errands, and when I was out, she confronted Al about the notes and was trying to tell him that I seemed unstable and egotistical, and that moving in was a bad idea. She showed him the notes, and he didn't really know what to make of them.

He asked me and I said that they were just some silly private notes to boost my self-confidence and make myself laugh; how had she gotten them? Had she been going through my things?

He said she was just tidying up and had seen them. And they were really weird.

I was like, "Have you met me?" You should know how weird I am. Anyway, if you don't want your mom to see my weird shit, you've got to stop letting her go through my shit. "

He asked if I left them on purpose to annoy her, and I admitted that was kind of the joke, but I also have other weird or private shit so what I said about her needing to stop snooping if she didn't want to find weird crap was still for real.

He said I was making stuff hard for him, his mom was really protective and adjusting to him moving in with a girlfriend for the first time, and I was agitating her on purpose and making her think I wouldn't be a good partner, when he wanted her to have the opposite impression of me!

So am I the Asshole?

38. I'M HIDING MY MONEY

I'm 16(m) and ever since I got a job my parents have been making me give them half my pay check for rent. I have 5 younger siblings and my parents said I had to start pulling my weight. It really sucks because they also want me to pay for stuff like new clothes and shoes. It was also like impossible to save. I really want my own car, and some for college.

When I got a raise at my job, I decided not to tell them. My pay went from 8/hr to 13/hr. I was so stoked, but I knew my parents would start making me pay them more, so I hid it. Because I choose to get paid by check, I just take it into the bank and cash it, so my parents won't be able to see the direct deposit. I can only work 20hrs a week because of school so before I could only save a little under $300 a month but now, I can save $600 a month. This has been going on for about 4-5 months.

The other day my mom found my savings and my parents confronted me. They could tell it was too much and made me show her my pay stub from the week before. To punish me for lying they took 3,000 of the 4,000 I had saved. Now I'm back at square one and won't be able to save as much.

So, I was talking to my cousins about the situation, and apparently one of them told my grandparents, and surprisingly, they reached out to my parents and talked to them. I don't know what my grandfather said exactly, but I was in my room doing school and all of a sudden, my mom walked in and put the cash down and told me not to keep secrets anymore and left. I counted it and it's the full $3,000.

39.THE GYM BUNNY

I (27 Female) have been married to my husband (34Male) for two years. we have two kids (11m, he's adopted and 1m). And he's a super fit guy. He likes to go camping, hiking swimming etc with our adopted son, I think that's why he wanted to adopt a kid to be honest.

I am not overweight or anything, but I'm not exactly in good shape. We tried to go on a family camping trip last fall but after about an hour I was just destroyed, and we had to go back to the car. I hate working out, I hate being sweaty and working hard. But he was really upset with me. He thought that I was keeping in shape during the day because I'm a stay at home mom, he doesn't understand how much work a baby is. He works in IT, so he spends all day sitting, not on his feet.

Now, I promised to get in better shape, so he started paying for a professional child career to come over and look after the baby for two hours a day to give me a break and signed me up for a gym. But after a month he came home angry and told me he talked to the gym, and they hadn't seen me come in once. I told him it was a mixed gym and I'm not comfortable working out around men. I promised him I'd join curves and actually work out and offered him he could track my phone to prove I was going. He already insists on tracking our older son's phone and lets me and our son track him. but I've always made excuses. I just think it's creepy and controlling.

So, I drive to the gym, and I think... I hate the gym. I hate working out, and I'm an adult god damn it! So, I just waited in my car.

sometimes I wait in the café next to the gym or something. But I just haven't gone to the gym at all for the last two months. And he keeps asking me how I'm feeling, and I keep saying it's great and I'm enjoying it. But yesterday he was waiting for me when I came home. he asked me how the gym was, and I said it was great. he asked if I have any problems and I said no. asked me if I showered at the gym and I said yeah, then he pulled out my gym bag. he took it out of my car two days ago. he realized I never washed my gym clothes.

He's pissed, says I lied to him. I told him he kept pressuring me and it's making me really uncomfortable. He' been sleeping in his home office for the last week. I don't get the big deal, I told him I'll go to the gym for real, but he says he doesn't care anymore and walks away.

 So am I the asshole?

40. THE YOGHURT COLLECTION

I'm a 29Female, my boyfriend is a 30Male. We've been living together for two years in a little studio in a very expensive, big US city.

My boyfriend grew up rurally, with lots of space, enough to collect all kinds of things. He collected action figures and video games and all the normal kids' stuff when he was young, but as he grew older, he became interested in more unusual things. As a teen, he had eight guinea pigs, of different types from different breeders. Since Tide Pods were released seven years ago, he's saved one of every kind of Tide Pod. He's got a big box of an international variety of electric insulators, those little ceramic hats that power lines wrap around on power poles.

He's not a hoarder. He's usually neat, just used to having lots of space for his bizarro collections. At his parents' ranch, he has two big rooms full of containers of weird (and impressive!) things.

He recently became interested in Yogurt. He's always hated dairy products, until about a year ago. He not just started drinking milk and sharing ice cream with me, but he's found a love for yogurts. So, he now collects them, of course. The problem is that they're perishable.

So, until earlier today, our little 550 sq. foot studio contained about 2100 cups of yogurt. It comes in tons of varieties. Different types, flavours, textures, containers, made by different companies in different countries. This is like crack to my boyfriend. So, he tried to pretty much save a sample of everything he could find.

He filled our fridge, bought a new fridge, and then another tiny bedside fridge (he said he didn't want to walk to the fridge at night, but it was obviously a ruse to get more yogurt space). These fridges all filled up with his yogurts, and if you keep them for long, they smell bad. Sometimes the packaging breaks. So, our apartment was smelling like rotten milk for the last two weeks -- and my boyfriend's attitude was "oh it's fine" and "just deal with it for a little longer" until I pulled the plug and threw it all out this morning. I was looking at my groceries, which I had to put beside the fridge because there was no space, and everything smelled like death, and then I kind of snapped and threw it all away.

My boyfriend is understandably upset. We've been arguing about whether I crossed a line by throwing away his stuff. And he's especially upset because he (of course) had rare yogurts that were hard to find -- in particular, he had some Cuban and Iranian yogurts that you can't get in the US. But I know that we have trade sanctions against Iran and Cuba, so I don't know if it was even legal for him to have them? I asked where he got his Iranian yogurt, but he kept insisting "the Iranian Yogurt is not the issue here" and that the real issue was me throwing out his precious yogurts without his permission.

So, I The Asshole?

41. THE OLIVES IN THE FRIDGE

My DH brought home a Metal box that he checks on often during the day when it's in the fridge. When asked about it, He said it had freshly picked olives his friend "Tony" got from his uncle's farm and wanted DH to keep till he gets back from his business trip. I had no problem with him keeping it safe at the bottom of the fridge. DH always asks me to be cautious with the box and not open it as it'd be rude to touch other people's stuff.

Yesterday I decided to clean out the fridge which took me about 2 hours from unplugging the fridge, emptying all items (groceries, vegetables and containers) and washing and cleaning out the inside of it then letting it settle before plugging it in again. I took the box my husband brought out the fridge and placed it on the kitchen island alongside other containers.

While I was working, I received a video call via WhatsApp from my husband while at work feeling bored asking what I was doing. I showed him I was cleaning out the fridge and he suddenly freaked out and asked about the metal box. I was confused so I told him to calm down and showed him where the box was. He got mad telling me I shouldn't have cleaned out the fridge nor even touched the box without telling him. I again tried to ask him to calm down as I saw no big deal with that. His precious box was safe and sound, but he went on a rant about how the box needed to be put back inside the fridge asap and told me to plug the fridge in right then, but I couldn't because it was wet and I still wasn't finished with cleaning other parts.

Apparently, I pissed him off by "stalling" and he hung up and 30minutes later he came home and pitched a hissy fit saying I should've picked a time where he was at home to clean out the fridge so he could take the box somewhere else to keep it cool. I said so what it was sitting out the fridge for barely 2hr and olives can stand being outside the fridge for longer period. He said I don't get it and took the box wanted to leave with it. I asked where he was taking it, he said he needed to go back to work and had no time to explain. I shrugged this whole thing off, but he came back with it in the evening and put it inside the fridge then complained about me cleaning the fridge without telling him and acting dismissive of his opinions. I argued what opinions could he have on cleaning out the fridge. He argued back saying he promised Tony he'd keep his olives in good condition and that I should've just told him, end of story.

I wonder if I messed up. He usually doesn't get that mad unless I've messed up and I think I have.

So am I the asshole?

42.MY BROTHER?

I've struggled with this for years (23Female). I have vague memories of a boy and when I remember the memories, I'm overcome with a sense of love and loss. When I was younger, thinking about him would make me cry.

When I was about 9, I found pictures of him and a family friend's son ("J") for the first time and was excited because I thought he'd been an imaginary friend since everyone acted like they didn't know who I was talking about. My mom said that one was J, but the boy I remembered, she didn't know, so it must have been his friend. I was content with this since I hung out with J all the time before we moved, and figured I'd met him then.

Years later when I was in high school, we moved in with my Granny because she got sick. She never let me see or touch her keys, and I figured it was because, as a kid, she was afraid of me losing them. One day though, her friend picked her up and she left her keys. There were those keychain kindergarten pictures you get from school photos- one of me, one of my little sister, and one of the boy. I was shocked, and when Granny got home, I asked her about it. She started *sobbing* but wouldn't talk for the rest of the night. The next day, she told me never to ask about him again.

Shortly after, she asked for help sorting through stuff. I found a box full of baby boy toys, and clothes that would fit a six or seven year old. Granny yanked the box away and told me she didn't need my help anymore and locked herself in her room. When she was well enough for us to move back home, I was helping my mom sort through pictures and found a whole rubber banded stack of photos of the boy from a few months old until third grade. Mom got very quiet but said she must have gotten them from the J's mom by mistake.

For years I've let it go, but recently I found more pictures that were mixed up in my baby book. They obviously got stuck and weren't meant to be there, but now I'm burning with curiosity. If I didn't have memories of him, I would say it's none of my business, but I *remember* this boy, and I know it can't be a cousin or a crazy young Uncle since Granny had a hysterectomy after Mom.

I think he either died in the fire that happened when I was 3-4, or he was born with a hereditary heart condition that almost killed my little sister. I don't want to bring up more pain, but I *remember* him, and for years I thought I imagined him. Don't I deserve an answer to my own memories? Or WIBTA for bringing up a potential death of my mom's child?

So am I the asshole?

43. WHO BLAMES A CAT?

My (29Female) husband Ted (34Male) and I have been together for 10 years. We met early in college and dated all throughout. I graduated before him and took a semester for travelling while he finished so we could move to another state, he ended up having to repeat some classes so when I came back we couldn't move yet and I had no place of my own, so I moved in with him and his roommate/brother Ash (32Male) while Ted finished school.

Before moving in I made sure that Ted cleared it with Ash that I was bringing my male cat with me. They had a dog who was old, but Ash said he was fine with it.

About 3 weeks after moving in I started noticing that our bedroom started to smell a lot like pee, and we couldn't figure out where it was coming from. My cat is toilet trained so I knew it wasn't him, and the dog couldn't go into our room because it was on the 2nd floor, and he had hip problems. I started finding clothes on the floor smelling like pee.

I asked Ted and he said he had no idea. After 3 months of frustration and this happening about 2x week I asked Ash if he was bringing the dog upstairs, he said no. At this point I'm fed up, I stopped leaving clothes anywhere, but I was still finding pee in my shoes, my throw pillows, things like that. After breaking down one day Ash suggested it was my cat marking his territory as male cats are known for doing that, he said it made sense as it was only on my things, and it was a new place.

I trust my cat with my whole heart, so I set up a camera in our room, I was paying rent, boyfriend knew about it, so I figured this was the way to find out where the pee was coming from. Lo and behold, Ash was coming into our room AND PEEING ON MY STUFF. When I saw the video, I packed my things and cat, and went to stay with a friend until Ted finished college and we moved. When all of this happened, I refused to confront him because EW and Ted dealt with that.

I haven't really spoken to Ash since, he was a best man at the wedding, but we tend to keep clear of each other at family gatherings and such. With the pandemic Ash lost his job and apartment and is honestly struggling financially. He asked if he could move in with us and I honestly don't want to because HE PEED ON MY STUFF. He was 25 years old when it happened, he was a grown ass man. Now their whole family is calling and texting telling me I'm an ass for leaving him homeless in the middle of a pandemic, but it wasn't Their things getting peed on.

SO am I the Asshole?

44. THE OVERBEARING MOTHER

I'm 36M and my wife is 28F. I've been married for 4 years, together for 6, and have a one-year-old daughter who is the light of my life. My wife is an amazing mother and partner. My own mother, on the other hand, is absolutely ridiculous and my wife has made me realise over time that my relationship with her is not healthy. My mom tries to control everything, including our wedding (which I convinced my wife to suck it up and go with my mom's ideas--she is still resentful of me for it). Passive aggressive behaviour on my mother's part, basically since we started dating, has made my wife absolutely hate her. I'll admit it. I haven't been as firm with my mom as I should have been in the past.

This brings us too yesterday. Our wedding anniversary was last night. We're a little tight on money right now, being new parents, and our jobs are not fantastic. So, I suggested that a family member watch our daughter while I went out and bought us a nice bottle of wine and we cooked dinner and just relaxed. I could tell my wife was disappointed that we couldn't do anything bigger or better, but she agreed that this was the best choice, and we settled to be home from work at 6 PM. I was headed home from work when I got a call from my mother asking me to come over because it was an "emergency". I asked her what type of emergency it was, and she just started crying frantically and begging me to come over. It was already 5:30 PM, but I live in a low-volume traffic area, so I figured I would stop by and calm my mom down before I met my wife. When I got to my mother's house, she was literally sitting on the couch having a glass of wine and watching TV. I was livid. She was so calm too, not the frantic monster I was speaking to on the phone. I started pressing about what the emergency was and reminded her that this was the night of my wedding anniversary, and she said she had some house tasks for me to do that, in my opinion, she was 100% capable of doing herself. Things like washing the dishes, watering her houseplants, cleaning the gutters, etc. So definitely not emergency material. But she guilted me into doing them (she was literally screaming at me at one point that I was a bad son) and I texted my wife, letting her know that I was going to be late because I was at my mom's house. She didn't respond to my text.

Before I knew it, it was 7:30 PM. My mom kept trying to put more tasks on me, but I put my foot down and let her know that I needed to get home. When I finally got home to my wife, she wasn't there. I was worried, so I texted and called her many times. No response. I was able to track her phone and found out that she was at her parents' house (they don't live far away, around 20 minutes away). She finally got back at 11:00 PM and as I greeted her with a glass of champagne, she told me to save it for myself because she wanted a divorce.

I was shocked and started breaking down. I asked her why, and she said that tonight was the final straw in a long list of things that I've always put my mother first. She said that she expected today of all days to be our one time together, but even my mom was able to intervene on our wedding anniversary. I asked her what I could do and begged her to go to counselling. She is refusing. I asked her if there was someone else. She said that someone else is herself, and that it's time for her to start working on herself and stop worrying about me being able to put my mother first. She has since moved into the guest bedroom in our house and hasn't talked to me much this morning. I tried to kiss her on the way out to drop off our daughter before work, and she just moved out of my way.

So, how do I save this sinking ship? I'm committed to doing everything for my wife to improve this, but she says that this is past fixing. I'm at a complete loss. I'm worried that she will see (or already has seen) a divorce lawyer, and I'd like to stop this in its tracks before it goes too far.

So am I the asshole?

45. AN UNFORTUNATE DEATH

Me (29Female) and my husband (32Male) had our daughter a few months ago. Due to complications, I had to have an emergency c-section and she had to be incubated for a few weeks as she was born prematurely. We weren't able to be by her side at all hours of the day and it was agony for us, and it has made me overly protective of her.

Eventually, she was strong enough to come home, and for the first two weeks of her being home, I was still recovering from her birth, and she was still so tiny and frail that we didn't go anywhere. We did have family members (in our bubble) come round to help out with housework, bring us meals occasionally, and do the usual, but they always came to us. We didn't go out and take the baby to visit people.

My Mother in law was a phenomenal woman who'd been battling bowel cancer for 3 years. Over the past year, her body had gotten progressively weaker, and she was essentially bedridden, but she was still very sharp mentally and was excited about welcoming her first grandchild into the world.

She was receiving care at home as they'd basically told us that there was nothing more, they could do aside from make her comfortable during the time she had left. We knew it was coming eventually, we just didn't know when.

My husband was eager to take our daughter over to his parents' house so they could meet her properly, but the thought of taking her on a trip that wasn't absolutely essential (i.e., healthcare related) made me anxious. I didn't go over to visit while I was recovering, but he visited Mother in law regularly alone-I was just apprehensive about him taking the baby and hated the thought of being apart from her again after what we'd been through, even though it'd only be for a few hours.

I told him that I wanted our little girl to meet her grandparents so much, just not yet-hang on a little bit longer.

Sadly, my Mother in law ended up passing away before we could take our daughter round to meet her. We are all heartbroken, and the grief has hit my husband hard. He's starting to resent that I "kept our daughter away from his mom" and he's become quite hostile towards me.

I feel guilty and selfish. There was no malicious intent behind it. I genuinely didn't think Mother in law would be taken from us so soon, and my mind was too focused on protecting our tiny baby. The more I think about it, the more I feel like I was overreacting, and now there's no way I can fix this. My husband has been sleeping in the spare room, and I feel like I've sabotaged the happiness we should be feeling as new parents.

My family and friends are on my side and say I couldn't have predicted the future, I was just doing what I thought was best and my husband is only acting this way because of grief, but I feel terrible, and I know I've made the process of losing his mom even harder than it would have been. My FIL is upset about it too, although he doesn't seem to blame me as much as my husband does.

SO am I the Asshole?

46. A POTLUCK WEDDING

We got married recently, and I wanted something super laid-back and casual. I hate a lot of things about wedding culture, so we decided to get married in a forest on some land my granddad owns. It turned out pretty well, except for the heat (we are going through a heat wave), but I was a little worried about my husband's side of the family complaining. They have more money than me and are used to nicer things. My Mother in law bitched about having to bring her own chair or blanket, but my husband shut that down at once.

Our rule was no set guest list. I don't care if extra people come, as long as they bring food and drinks. It was a potluck, and we asked for food instead of gifts. The more food you have, the more tag-alongs you can bring. She gave us a gift card to a grocery/liquor store for a couple hundred, brought a couple boxes of desserts from a local bakery, and brought a giant vat of this amazing pasta salad she makes, so she was totally in the clear to bring some people. She came with her boyfriend, his brother, who was in town visiting, his brother's wife, and a friend.

When Mother in law got there, she asked my mom about where to put things and wasn't happy with our accommodations. My mom thought it was unsanitary that we had no way of keeping food cold, but my mom told her it would be an hour at the most and it was fine. Mother in law also claims there were flies getting into other people's food, but I was getting dressed and didn't see that. Now, for some context, this pasta salad that my mother-in-law makes is one of my all-time favourite dishes.

During the ceremony, I looked over and her boyfriend and her friend were eating some of the pasta salad out of the container. That is obviously unsanitary, so I confronted them right after, and her BF said he really wanted some and didn't want to "die" after leaving it in the provided "conditions." Now her boyfriend is typically a drama queen, so I wasn't surprised, but angry and disappointed. I said since bringing people was linked to bringing food, the two of them had to leave because they were taking away from the food supply. My Mother in law got mad and said I was ruining her son's wedding for her. They ended up not leaving because my granddad wouldn't kick them out. My mom even took Mother in law's side and said I was causing a scene. There is still annoyance on both ends, so I just wanted some clarity.

So am I the asshole?

47. THE VACATION

Hello, my girlfriend, myself, my parents, and my brother and his wife went on vacation in another country a week ago. My brother and I were the ones who did most of the planning of the itinerary, although we did ask everyone else for input. For background, I make around $150,000k as an IT consultant, and my girlfriend is a teacher, making $45,000k. My parents are pretty affluent, as are my brother and sister-in-law.

My girlfriend knew this trip was coming up and took on a second job waitressing on the weekends for several months to get ready for it. We have always split things 50/50 in the 2 years we have been together. There were a few times on the vacation when she did not go on outings with us, like wine tasting, scuba diving, etc. She also only ate 2 meals a day, simply stating that she was on a budget. My family does favour more expensive (*expensive*) places. My parents thought it was very strange that she only eats 2 meals a day, although normally she eats 3.

When we got home, I asked her why she skipped out on several of the outings and only ate 2 meals a day. I mentioned how I heard her stomach growling one night and said I was concerned about her having an eating disorder. She got teary-eyed and said that 3 meals a day wasn't fiscally feasible for her, and neither were the outings that she chose not to go on (she went on 3 of 6 outings). She said she was not expecting everything to cost so much, and she was overwhelmed.

She also said she doesn't know if this is going to work long-term if she is expected to go on vacations like that with people who make so much more than her. I feel bad that I did not pick up on her discomfort sooner. But we did agree to split everything 50/50, and I don't know why she agreed to come if the cost was an issue.

So am I the asshole?

48.MY WIFE THE FEMINIST

My daughter is 13. I am married to my wife who has very feminist values. I also have my parents who are very traditional. My parents are extremely strict and can come off as cold but deep down they are loving, they don't show it as much. They are the authoritarian type, just like when I was growing up, but I learned to respect my parents even if I was unhappy with them, and I'm a stronger person for it.

I know my parents don't like my wife, and they make it very clear. If she had her way, she would cut them off from us, and I know how unhappy they make her, but they are my parents, and I would never abandon them.

My daughter has made it clear since the time she was little that she hates my parents. She would cry and refuse to get in the car to go see them, so I would have them over.

They aren't cruel but they will put their foot down when my daughter acts up. They don't let her speak unless she is spoken to first. They often judge what my daughter wears and does.

I usually have them over when my wife is at work, so she won't speak up about them like she has in the past. I know my daughter doesn't like it, but I want her to at least be able to see her grandparents, and I hope she will be glad she did.

Yesterday, my daughter revealed to my wife that for the past few years, I have been having my parents over a few times a month.

My wife originally thought I was having them over only once a month and wasn't making our daughter have anything to do with them.

My wife is pissed that I have been lying to her, which I understand. But now she's telling me to cut off all contact with my parents and never bring them around again. Despite their flaws, I deeply respect and love my parents.

My daughter chimed in, sobbing and saying that I should put my parents in a nursing home and leave them to die. When they die, she will stomp and dance on their grave.

I'm at a crossroads right now. My wife and daughter are sobbing and pissed at me and want me to abandon my parents, the people who gave me life and shaped me into the man I am today.

So am I the Asshole

49.THE TWINS

My sister, 36, has four teenage kids, all boys. The youngest two are a pair of fraternal twins (Alex and Bryan), now 14. My sister has been regularly sending the twins over to my place whenever she needs a break since I moved near her two years ago.

I (26Female) do not have kids myself, but I love having them over. I'm particularly fond of them as I grew up babysitting the four boys for loads of spare cash. $$$$

The only issue is that Alex is clearly my sister's favourite child. And everyone is aware of this. To be fair, he is the stereotypical "good" kid-extremely smart, good looking, well spoken, and charismatic. Everyone loves him. Bryan is more quiet, meek, and less blessed in the looks department, but he is not a bad kid at all.

But I seriously think there's a cruel streak in Alex. I caught Alex "daring" Bryan drinking pee when they were 9. In quotes because Bryan confessed that Alex threatened to cut him out of their friend group if he didn't do it. I've personally heard Alex's horrible comments about Bryan's weight, looks, intelligence, etc. when he thinks I can't hear them. Bryan has also shared that Alex has been vandalising his belongings, spreading horrible rumours at school.

My sister absolutely refuses to punish Alex or send him to any sort of therapist or professional who can help. She says it's just boys being boys. And it is not my place to override her parenting decisions.

So, I've been trying to "balance" out the favouritism while they are at my house. I usually ask Bryan for his preferences on minor things, like picking out the dinner that I cook for them or the movies that we watch together. If Alex makes snide remarks, I shut it down at once.

But the more I speak up for Bryan, the angrier Alex gets. It has gotten to the point where Bryan just defers to Alex's preferences and asks me to get off this so that Alex doesn't take it out on him when they get home.

I get where Bryan is coming from, but I can't just let this go. My sister doesn't do anything about it.

So, Reddit, SO am I the Asshole for treating my nephews differently AND not stopping even though they both want me to?

So am I the asshole?

49.THE NEIGHBOURS KIDS

I (35Female) just moved with my husband (43 Male) and our dog, who is a Pitbull mix and who has never had an actual yard to play in. We got him when we still lived in an apartment, and needless to say, he's having the time of his life out there. The problem is that we have neighbours, a spouses with four kids, all of whom are quite young, and our dog barks incessantly whenever they're in the yard at the same time.

I talked to my husband and decided to ask the parents if they could prevent the children from going outside at certain times that our dog was out there, but the wife told me that it was ridiculous and that I shouldn't expect them to keep their kids inside just because our dog isn't trained.

That set me off and I snapped at him and told him that that was uncalled for and that he had to compromise a little bit, but the husband stepped in and said that he understands the predicament but that his wife is right and that I shouldn't expect them to bend over backwards just because our dog isn't trained, and then they shut the door.

So am I the asshole?

50.PARENTING MY 18-YEAR-OLD

Am I (37Female) an asshole for refusing to remove parental controls from my daughter's (17Female) electronic devices, even after she's an adult?

All of my kids (17F, 15M, and 10Female) have parental controls enabled on their devices, and I have a device that limits their internet access. The controls restrict the internet and apps—specifically the content they can access, the maximum time they can use apps/games/internet and set a bedtime (8 pm) where all the internet and most apps turn off. For a 17-year-old, she has fairly relaxed controls; the main thing is that they turn off at night (8 pm) and there are time limits. I do NOT look at what websites she visits or anything like that, and she can access social media, texting, FaceTime, etc. I do sometimes restrict her access if she has late homework, doesn't do her chores (like multiple days in a row), or otherwise misbehaves, but this is rare.

She asked if I could take them off of her devices when she turned 17, so we did a trial. She has a history of depression (we started using parental controls like this when she was in therapy under the advisement of her treatment team), and over the five weeks she had them disabled, she began isolating, staying up all night, not doing things she enjoys, and falling asleep in online classes. I put them back on, had her go back to see her therapist, and she quickly went back to her old self (straight A student who is asleep by 10, reads multiple books a week, runs track and cross country, volunteers, and plays in the orchestra). She contends that I overreacted, and she was fine.

She brought it back up this week. She will be attending college part-time in the fall (morning will be high school classes, afternoon will be college classes) and turn 18 in December.

After putting some thought into it, I told her I would be willing to negotiate some changes (like a later "bedtime") but that as long as I was paying for her internet and cell phone, I would continue to use the controls, even after she turns 18, if I felt she needed them. Of course, she is free to pay for her own internet or phone plan, but as she currently doesn't work for pay, this isn't an option.

She is very angry with me and feels I am infantilizing her. She even called my sister to ask if she could move in with her.

SO am I the Asshole?

51. MY DAUGHTER THE READER

My daughter Rose (9) is a very advanced reader. She's in 3rd grade (8–9 year olds) but reads at a 9th grade (14–15 year old) level.

Despite her advanced reading level, the only books she wants to read are the I Survived series and the A-Z mysteries. Both of these books are far below her reading level, so I told her it's fine if she wants to read them in school, but at home she has to read things closer to her level.

I've taken her to bookstores, and we've looked through the young adult section, but she refuses to read any of the books. She says they're all boring and gross. She always asks to get books from the children's section, but I've said no because they're too easy for her.

Rose has started sneaking books home from school, and when I started taking those away, she stopped reading in general. Rose has now pulled away from me, and her teacher is recommending that I let her read whatever she wants.

Rose's dad (my ex) found out about this and tore into me for not letting Rose read books for kids her age. He offered to send her books, but that's not the problem. I don't have a problem with Rose reading, but if she's going to read, she should read something close to her level.

So am I the asshole?

52. MY FRIENDS' BABY

This is what happened. My friend (29Female) was talking with someone at the door and was away from the baby (I don't know how old the baby is, but it can't walk yet) for like 40 minutes. She trusted me to keep an eye on the baby while she talked, she trusted me to keep an eye on the baby while she talked. The baby was crying and hollering, so I assumed it was hungry or thirsty.

I didn't want to just go into my friend's refrigerator without her permission. I was drinking a bottle of Sprite at the time, and I began giving the baby small sips, the baby quieted down.

My friend comes into the room and sees me and the child and goes ballistic and starts cussing me out. I told her it was no big deal, and she was gone for a while, and she told me to get out. I've been trying to apologize, but she won't accept it. This is spiralling into her making jabs at me on Facebook. Calling people who take care of other people's kids retarded It seems as though that was it for our friendship.

So am I the Asshole?

53.MY GRANDPARENTS

I (21 Male) am getting married this summer. I am straight; my fiancée is a woman, obviously. I have two older cousins (29Male and 26Female), let's call them Mark and Jane, both of whom are openly gay and lesbian, respectively.

My grandparents (87Male and 79Female) are unashamedly homophobic. They have attended every straight wedding in the family. They declined invitations to Mark and Jane's weddings because they "don't believe that's a real marriage."

Here's the problem: Homophobia aside, my grandparents are amazing, hard-working, good people. I intend to invite them to my own wedding. Jane and Mark completely oppose this. Because I'm a bit of a "golden boy" for the family, they want me to exclude my grandparents from my wedding to punish them and to "promote marriage equality." I refuse to listen to them.

Most of the family has taken my side (it's a very big family), except for Jane, Mark, their in-laws, and Mark's parents. They call me a homophobe and a terrible person or beg me not to invite my grandparents. I won't listen to them, but I feel somewhat sorry that I'm not fighting my grandparents for them.

So am I the Asshole

54. THE WEDDING BREAKFASTS

My sister "Jess" (30 Female) got married on Saturday morning. I (26 Female) did not attend for a multitude of reasons, but primarily because I don't care for her fiancé, "Jay," and we don't get along, so I figured I would skip to allow for them to have a happy time without me being a Debbie downer and raining on their parade.

Due to the wedding, several family members were in town, some of whom I hadn't seen for quite a few years and may not get to see again before they get too old or pass away as they are older or live out of the country.

Since I didn't go to the wedding, I figured that I would host a family dinner later in the evening, as most family members were scheduled to leave on Sunday or Monday, and everyone would be split up.

The wedding began at 11 a.m. and the dinner was scheduled to begin at 5 p.m. I do live about an hour from the venue, so I knew most people would be on the road by 4 pm, but I figured that seeing as the wedding started at 11, 5 hours would be plenty of time for everyone to visit and mingle with Jess at the actual wedding.

At around 4:30, Jess called me, completely irate, yelling, swearing, and just generally saying harsh things about how I'd stolen her guests and ruined her day in multiple ways, especially since I didn't invite her and Jay to the dinner (again, the fiancé that I don't get along with).

I didn't beg anyone to come to the dinner, nor did I pressure anyone, and I left it open to them all to decide whether or not they wanted to come (which most of them did). I thought this was a fine compromise since it would decrease the tension for everyone involved and make for smoother sailing, but Jess sent me an incredibly nasty message and has blocked me from her Instagram and Facebook. I'm unsure of whether or not she blocked my phone number or if she's just not responding.

I didn't think the dinner idea was so terrible, but my boyfriend feels like it was an a-hole move and that I should try and apologise to her, but I need more perspectives.

So am I the Asshole?

55.THE SISTERS' WEDDINGS

My daughter has always been resentful of my stepdaughter, and growing up, we've had to deal with a lot of issues related to this resentment.

The unfortunate reality was that my ex and I had shared custody, so naturally, I saw my daughter less than my stepdaughter. My stepdaughter's biological father passed away, and I've treated her like my own since she was 2. I love them both equally and I've never shown preferential treatment towards my stepdaughter, something my daughter always accuses me of.

In 2019, my stepdaughter sent out a save the date for her wedding on a Saturday in September. My daughter at once called me, furious and accusing her stepsister of deliberately planning her wedding the day before hers.

My daughter sent her own save the date a week later for the Sunday of that same weekend.

I talked to my stepdaughter, who said it was pure coincidence and that she doesn't even talk to my daughter after all those years of them not getting along.

The issue was that my daughter's wedding was happening in another state that was a 13-hour drive away.

And both of them wanted me to walk them down the aisle.

All of my extended family chose to attend my daughter's wedding over my stepdaughter's.

I did the math and calculated that if I left my stepdaughter's wedding at 10pm and drove through the night, I'd make it with 2 hours to freshen up and get ready.

Unfortunately, I got lost along the way, plus traffic, and I missed the actual wedding ceremony. My daughter's stepfather ended up walking her down the aisle by himself.

I feel like I tried my best to make both my children happy, but I completely failed one of them. My stepdaughter and her husband have been attacked on Facebook by my daughter's friends, who are claiming that my stepdaughter planned it on purpose.

And when I tried to clear up the situation, I was completely shut down.

I gave my daughter and son-in-law an added gift of money to go to Japan, which has always been their dream. It was a lot of money, but I hoped it would be a sort of way for me to ask for forgiveness.

They had to postpone their trip because of Covid, but my daughter refuses to even consider any sort of forgiveness.

The few times she picks up my calls, it always ends with her bringing up the wedding and getting angry at me again.

I was told by a few members of my family that I was an asshole for not prioritising my biological child's wedding and skipping my stepdaughter's wedding instead.

SO am I the Asshole?

56. UNEQUAL PUNISHMENTS

Myself, my wife, and my two daughters, Abby (23) and Sophie (17), went out for a meal.

Sophie has suffered from some food and body image issues in the past and is in a much better place now. When she took her part, Abby loudly said, "Do you need to eat that much?" Sophie was obviously upset. In fact, she pushed the food away and left the table in tears. My wife had to follow her and comfort her. I demanded why Abby made such a cruel comment when she knows what Sophie has been through in the past, but she just shrugged her shoulders and laughed.

For Abby's last birthday, we bought her an engraved bracelet and matching earrings, which were very expensive. She loves them and wears them often.

When we got home, Abby went for a shower. She came down later and said she couldn't find her bracelet or earrings. We helped her search and practically turned the house upside down. We couldn't find them, and Abby wanted to try Sophie's room. Sophie loudly refused, but we had to try. We found the jewellery. Sophie started to cry and said she took it to "teach Abby a lesson".

We've had to punish Sophie. We've put her on laundry and cleaning duty for the next two weeks.

My wife thinks we should punish Abby too because of her cruel comment to Sophie. She thinks we should confiscate the jewellery. I get the idea, but Abby is an adult with a professional career. We can't simply confiscate a gift that she now owns like we would if she was a kid.

Also, taking the jewellery would achieve what Sophie wanted in the first place. Should we really be teaching her that stealing is, OK? Especially for extremely valuable items?

I've been thinking about this for hours. I know what Abby said was awful, but the punishment my wife wants is inappropriate and will reward stealing.

So am I the Asshole?

57.THE HEIRLOOM

Honestly, COVID-19 hit me (34Male) and my wife (32Female) pretty hard. I was let down, and my wife's salary isn't sufficient to support both of us and our son (3). We resorted to selling a couple of our most important possessions to make ends meet. My wife and I had both decided our marriage meant more than her wedding ring; we decided to pawn it and received a sufficient amount. The ring was a gift from my grandmother before she passed away and meant a lot to her. However, extraordinary circumstances call for extraordinary measures. This was difficult for the both of us, but in the end, it helped us a lot. Fast forward to last week (I sold it around 8 months ago). I was on our weekly zoom calls with my extended family, and my mother casually mentioned the ring to my sister, who is currently ring-shopping and preparing to get married in the fall. She asked my wife to show it to her again, which called for a very awkward pause. We knew we'd have to tell them some day and eventually let it out. My mother and sister were livid. My sister screamed at my wife and said she would've just asked our grandmother for the ring for herself if she knew we'd sell it. We told her it was a dire situation and, technically, we'd received it as a gift, granting us the ability to sell it if we wanted to. Apparently, the ring meant more to my mother than anyone else. I had no idea what it meant, let alone that it was considered "the family heirloom. "If I had known, my wife and I would have reconsidered selling it.

My sister called a couple days later and apologised and said she knew we were in a rough patch and how difficult it was for us. She asked why we didn't loan the money from her, and honestly it did cross our mind but the feeling of remaining debt-free was too good to pass. My wife and I have been in financial trouble earlier where my sister's fiancé had helped us, we paid him back as soon as we could, but I still feel our relationship has been awkward ever since. My mother, however, is demanding we go back to the pawn shop and try to buy it from them. Since I was let down, I received another job offer and am making around 1.5x as much as I did earlier. Honestly, we're financially stable enough to rebuy the ring, my sister even contacted the shop and they said they still have it available for purchase. But we made the conscious choice to sell it and told her we refuse to rebuy it. I feel kind of bad, but it was still a gift to us. Selling it was more symbolic than anything and deeply strengthened me and my wife's relationship.

So am I the asshole?

58.MY WIFE AND DAUGHTER

My wife and I have a daughter, Ava (13). My wife is a great mom and takes good care of Ava, but lately I feel like she's spoiling Ava and not letting her be as independent as she should be.

Some examples of this are: Ava struggles in school, so my wife emails all of Ava's teachers to ask for modified assignments (she has an IEP, which I feel is unneeded, but that's a different story) and sits down with her every day after school to do homework with her or do projects with her or study for tests. I don't think Ava has done a single assignment alone this year.

Then today, Ava assumed the weather would be like yesterday (50 degrees and windy), so she dressed for that weather without checking the weather app on her phone or tablet. Today was 80 degrees and sunny, so my wife ended up sending cold water bottles to Ava's classes and made her spend recess and lunch inside (my wife is a teacher at that school, so that's how she was able to do that) so she "wouldn't get heat stroke". It was only 80 degrees outside, and the lunch tables were all in the shade, so Ava would've been fine outside.

Even an hour ago, Ava came to us and said that her head hurt, and she was nauseous, so my wife was in Ava's room rubbing her back to "comfort her". Over a damn headache.

In my opinion, Ava needs to learn how to function on her own, so I told my wife to stop babying Ava and to let her take care of herself. She can study for a test by herself or take a Tylenol and go to bed without mommy being there to hold her hand, rub her back, and stop trying to get Ava out of situations like today. She can deal with being a little hot for a couple of hours and learn to check the weather app in the mornings.

Well, now my wife is refusing to talk to me and is planning on sleeping in the guest room tonight.

So am I the asshole?

59.THE FERTILITY PROCEDURE

My eldest son is 37 and married to my daughter-in-law, who is also 37. Three months ago, they both came over and told my wife and I that they had done two rounds of IVF, but unfortunately, neither was successful and they needed some money so they could secure another round of IVF with an egg donor this time. Obviously, my wife and I were glad to offer help and fortunately had some money we could give. However, given the short notice, the total was still short, which brought me to the decision to sell my old Boxster since I didn't use it anymore and have another car. I managed to sell it to an old friend and had more than enough for my DIL's fertility treatment. For those interested, it was thankfully a success, they're both excited and the pregnancy has been going well.

The problem is that my youngest daughter, who is 19, found out that I sold the Porsche in order to help and was extremely upset with me. I didn't understand why until she told me that I'd apparently promised her when she was 14 that the Porsche would be hers after she got her degree. She's never mentioned this before and I don't recall it happening, but I probably did, so I apologised and promised to just buy her another car then, or even another Boxster. However, she's still not happy with me and told me to just forget it. Even if I remembered, the time sensitivity of my son and DIL's situations would've taken preference because my daughter still has a few years until then and I'd be able to buy another car for her.

JAMIE GOLDSON

Am I the Asshole?

60.THE DIAGNOSES

My daughter is 21 years old and has been diagnosed with BPD and Bipolar 2. She is currently medicated and going to therapy. But she often has huge meltdowns whenever any minor inconvenience goes on in her life. Her meltdowns often consist of full mental breakdowns with crying, screaming, and pure rage.

Yesterday afternoon, she called me in the middle of one of her episodes. She had gotten a flat tyre on the interstate and was crying and screaming because she was frustrated that she wasn't strong enough to change it. She begged me to come help her, but I declined because I had an incredibly important call in 30 minutes, and she was 30 minutes away.

I told her to call her boyfriend, and she said she didn't want to bother him. I told her she'd have to figure it out on her own and not bother her stepfather like she usually does when I'm unable to assist her. We ended up getting into a huge argument while she was screaming and crying, telling me I didn't care about her. I just told her that she's too overly dependent on her stepfather and me and she needs to learn to handle her own issues for once in her life! She finally just hung up on me.

15 minutes later, my husband calls me and asks why I wouldn't go help our daughter. I tell him I'm busy. He then asks why I would tell her not to call him and I say it's because she always stresses him out and she needs to be a grown up and stop expecting us to fix everything.

He went ahead to get very mad at me as well and told me I had no empathy for her sometimes. I just told him that if he wants to continue to enable her bad behaviour that's up to him. They are both now ignoring me.

So am I the Asshole?

61. THE HOUSE RULES

My kids are 17, 14, and 8. The 8 year old doesn't have a phone but my two teens do. The rules are that they are not allowed to have their phone in the bedroom alone or bathroom during any time of the day, and at night they bring us (me and their dad) their phones and we lock them up. These rules are mostly because I know how vile the internet can be. I've had my younger siblings who grew up during the rise of the internet tell me horror stories, as well I very clearly remember the things I saw on the internet as an adult. I really don't want to risk any of these issues with my kids, as well it helps them not procrastinate homework or chores and we spend a lot more family time together.

This past week, my oldest had a new friend come over. The girls were going to my daughter's room, and so I asked for their phones. My daughter looked embarrassed but handed over her phone. Her friend then asked me what I meant. When I told her about my rule, she said she wanted to keep her phone. I then told them that they could stay in the living room. The girl got a little bit irritated, but they ended up staying out in the living room. The hangout then turned into a sleepover, and I called the kid's dad and talked to him a bit about our rules. The dad was a little bit sceptic about our rules (we get that often) but agreed. He told me he would relay this information to the mom as she was working.

Night-time came and everyone gave me their phones, except for my daughter's friend. She said that she felt more comfortable keeping her phone in case of an emergency. I told her if there was an emergency, she could come wake me and my husband up. She then told me she really didn't feel comfortable with that in case she wanted to text her mom to sleep. I told her if that was the case, she needed to just go home, because in our house the rule is no phones in the bedroom, period.

She called her mom in another room. I could hear her crying, and while I felt bad, I stood my ground. The mom apparently had just gotten off of work and had not talked to Dad and thought our phone rules were "creepy" and "invasive" and told me just that when she got to my house. She said that I should have just let her daughter keep her phone, and I told her that her daughter needed to follow my rules.

My oldest is now embarrassed and really upset with me, and even my husband thinks I should have relaxed a little more. I don't think I did anything wrong.

So am I the asshole?

62.THE HOLIDAY

Most of my siblings have kids, and we wanted to do something special for them after the pandemic ended. I pitched taking them all to Disney land since my kids love it and their kids have never been. Normally they couldn't afford the trip, but I decided to pitch in and help them out - I feel like my little nieces/nephews deserved it after being cooped up inside for a year. My childfree sister was also invited but she couldn't afford it.

She found out I was helping the others and asked if I could help her out as well - which I declined. She's been bitter towards me since, saying I was trying to exclude her from the family, etc. Am I the Asshole for not wanting to pay all this extra money to bring her on a trip to Disneyland meant for the children - she doesn't even like hanging out with kids? I'm fine if she comes but I just don't want to pay for it.

I am paying for my nieces and nephews by splitting the trip cost 50/50 with each of my siblings. I pitched this as a vacation to cheer up the kids after they've been stuck inside all year because of the pandemic.

So am I the Asshole?

63.THE COLLAGE

My older daughter Heather (15) doesn't like her sister Olivia (5) due to the age gap. My husband and I have tried everything to get them to bond, especially since Olivia looks up to her big sister. But nothing is working, and Heather just wants to stay away from her sister and for her sister to stay away from her.

It was Olivia's birthday yesterday, but since it was a school day and because of the pandemic, we couldn't give her a party. Instead, just a cake and family dinner. Heather took part without any hiccups, and then went to her room to make her wall collage.

Olivia wanted to play with her sister and went into her room. Heather was taping some pictures to her wall, and Olivia wanted to help. Heather reluctantly let her tape a couple of the pictures on the wall, but when Olivia started to accidentally crumple a couple of the paper cut-outs Heather was taping to her wall, she yelled at her sister to go away and stop ruining her stuff.

I wasn't too far away so I knew what the girls were doing. I at once went to scold Heather for being mean to her sister on her birthday. She told me that I always turned a blind eye to her sister encroaching upon her personal space and that she was done pampering the baby, who isn't even a baby anymore.

I told Heather that family doesn't have boundaries and that she had to be nicer to her sister, who only wanted her love and affection. Heather rolled her eyes and said she never asked for such a large age gap. I told her that her paper cut-outs were temporary, but family is forever.

My husband and I tried to make the rest of Olivia's birthday a good one, and we took down Heather's pictures from her wall collage as punishment. But was that an AH move? We know Heather is just an angsty teen, but we've had enough with the way she treats her sister.

So am I the Asshole

64.THE WATER BOTTLE

 My daughter (14) chews on everything, especially anything made of silicone. She has anxiety and sensory issues, so I think that's why she chews on stuff.

In June, I got her a water bottle, and it had a silicone straw lid. I didn't think anything of it because she's never broken anything that she's chewed on before. Last week, she came up to me and said that she chewed through the straw on her water bottle and asked me to take her to buy her a new one. I said no and that she could use one of her sister's bottles (she bought 3 water bottles and covered them in stickers. She doesn't mind people borrowing them until she buys herself a new one. She threw a tantrum because "she hates the way the stickers feel on her hands," and I told her she should've thought of that before she broke hers and sent her to her room until dinner.

She called her dad (my ex) and told him what happened and that she "can't drink water at school because of me" (she refuses to take plastic bottles too and the water fountains at her school are shut off due to covid) and when he picked her up yesterday he told the kids to leave the room and berated me for not buying her a new water bottle and wants to go to court to get full custody over this. He completely undermined my parenting and bought her 2 water bottles with replacement caps and some necklaces for her to chew on (I already told her that I don't want her wearing those). My daughter said she doesn't plan on coming home when her dad's custody time is up, so I wanted to see if I was wrong.

So am I the asshole?

65. IT'S NOT ABOUT HER.

I have a 28-year-old daughter and a 33-year-old son.

I remarried one year ago to my wife (30Female), and I had told her while dating that I was in my sixties and wasn't aiming to have more kids.

For the past few weeks, my wife has started acting strange and said she felt sick and tired.

The other day, my wife and I were visiting my daughter and her boyfriend, who had just gotten an apartment together. My wife was on edge the whole time. Finally, she blurted out that she had found out that she was pregnant.

She looked apprehensive, so I asked why she was treating this like bad news. She said she wasn't sure how I'd feel about the news. So, I told her that it was unexpected but that, especially recently, I've come to really value children in a way that I couldn't when I was younger and was either away from home altogether or working 13-hour days, six days a week.

I told her that my business is very much hands-off now and that this time around I have time and resources and am so excited to devote that to our child. And that I would do everything to make our child the happiest child in the happiest family.

My daughter was in the adjacent room, but I didn't notice that she had walked in. She started sniffing and when I asked what's wrong, she started full on crying.

She curtly said, "Congratulations" and started walking out.

I caught up with her in the hallway and she spun around and said " Great to see that you've finally calmed down dad- if only it happened 25 years ago and not just because of age."

I told her that I was only trying to make my wife feel better and that she didn't have to cry and yell because this wasn't about her. This was about letting an anxious woman I loved know that she and her child would want for nothing and worry about nothing.

She looked furious and said " Yeah- this is about a kid who is going to get a chill, indulgent dad and a happy mom because he got him the second time around."

After that, my wife and I left because we knew we weren't welcome at the moment.

 So am I the asshole?

66. THE INVESTMENT

My son was born in 2000 and I shortly afterwards opened up an investment account with the intentions of handing it off to him after he graduated college to give him a head start in life. Wife loved the idea!

I put in $10K initially and started adding $100/monthly and the account sits at over $60K today. A majority of it was just put into mutual funds and some months I'd take the $100 and toss it into riskier stocks that didn't really pan out. (Yes, I learned my lesson that if you're not making this a career, just toss it into funds)

When our daughter was born two years later, I started up an account for her as well. About a year later, my wife and I got drunk with friends and the topic of investing came up. Wife said something silly along the lines of "anybody can invest" and it became a lengthy discussion at the beach with all our friends chiming in. In the end, wanted to take over daughters investment account and manage it to show me how easy investing was. We discussed it at length over the following weeks and she dug her heels in, so I relented and gave her control.

Long storey short, that account sits at just over $16K for two reasons: because she picked (bad) individual stocks instead of funds and she wasn't adding to the account at the start of the month.

Well, we had a blowout fight about a week ago after I mentioned to our son that he was going to inherit a bunch of money once he graduates this spring. Naturally, our daughter wanted to know if and how much she was going to receive. I mentioned that of course I'd done the same for her, but she'd have to ask mom as I wasn't about to be the one to set that ticking time bomb off. After wife showed the numbers, the meltdown happened and then she told our daughter we'd just combine the accounts and split them equally. At this point I flipped a lid and explained we'd definitely not do that because in her "everybody can invest" BS she'd insulted how difficult investing was and needed to deal with the ramifications of poor choices in investing.

We've not had a meaningful discussion since, we've been cold to one another since, and our daughter is mad at us for the significantly smaller account she stands to inherit.

So am I the Asshole?

67. MY DAUGHTERS' FIGHT

My wife and I have two daughters. Laura (20) and Lily (15). Laura studying away but came home for the weekend.

Lily has just had her first boyfriend breakup and it's hit her hard. She's been crying in her room the past few days.

Unfortunately, Laura has a bit of a windup personality and was tormenting her little sister about the breakup, which only upset Lily more. She was saying things like if the boyfriend left her for "a prettier girl" and saying she "didn't blame him" etc. Horrible things. We did tell Laura repeatedly to cut it out, but she didn't listen, to the point that Lily went to bed in tears.

Laura has eye problems. She has been very visually impaired since she was a baby. Her current glasses prescription is -28 and she can't wear contacts.

We woke up this morning to screaming from Laura's room. Laura had woken up and put her glasses on, but the lenses had been popped out. Lily admitted to doing it and said she threw the lenses out the window. We did try to search for them outside, but they couldn't be found.

Laura was crying her eyes out and couldn't see anything at all. She does have a spare pair of glasses, but as she only came for a couple of days, she didn't bring them with her.

To be fair Lily regretted what she did as soon as she saw how upset Laura was, but Laura didn't want Lily near her and begged us to keep her away.

My wife's sister lives nearby, and I asked Lily to go and spend the day there, because Laura was blinded and looking after her had to be our main concern.

I then got a call from my SIL, saying "how dare you" throw her out for "that spoiled bully". It's not about spoiling anyone. Laura was blinded and terrified and was too scared to be in the same house as Lily. It was right to ask her to leave until we could get Laura back to her place where her spare glasses were.

I do get that it was harsh to just tell Lily to leave, but what else could we have done when our other child was unable to see and crying in fear?

So am I the asshole?

68.THE INVITATION

I'm engaged to the love of my life. We'll call her Sarah. Sarah doesn't have issues with my parents but there is a little tension on both sides, and no one has attempted to be close, which is fine, I guess. It makes me a little sad that they are not more excited about her.

Sarah asked my mom the other day if she would help make centrepieces. Sarah is into DIY, but we are running out of time, and she was asking around to see who would be willing to help. She admitted to my mom that it was kind of grunt work and if she didn't want to, no pressure. My mom got offended and said of course she doesn't want to, we haven't cared about her at all, so she doesn't care about our fucking wedding. This hurt Sarah but she didn't fight back.

Sarah told me and I called my mom. Honestly, I probably went into it a big aggressively, but I yelled at her for saying that to Sarah. My mom said that Sarah hasn't included her in any of the fun parts, or cared about her opinion on anything, so why would she help make centrepieces. I asked her to apologise to Sarah and my mom said no, she was done talking about it, so I uninvited her to the wedding.

My dad sent me a text, because I said he could still come, and pretty much told me to fuck off if I thought he would come without my mom. My mom is now upset because everyone is going to ask where she is. Sarah is very happy and feels like I defended her, and literally everyone else thinks I'm the asshole.

So am I the asshole?

69.MY MOTHER IN LAW

We are very low contact with my in laws. We might occasionally see them at a mutual family member's event, but there is no relationship. Mother in law chose to be low/almost no contact with us and then due to an issue around the wedding (she didn't come, FIL lied about why, I corrected him in front of the guests) FIL cut us off completely and said he didn't want a relationship anymore.

We saw them the other night for the first time in probably a year at a cousin's wedding. As they were leaving, Mother in law went to kiss SIL's son goodbye, which prompted my nephew asking why Mother in law never interacts with my kids. My 5 year old daughter said Mother in law isn't her grandmother, and her grandmother is her nana, meaning my mom. My nephew is a bit older and gets family relationships and said Mother in law is both of their grandmother.

Mother in law told my daughter that she chooses not to have a relationship with us, because we really hurt her husband. I only heard the end of this conversation, but SIL filled me in. I asked Mother in law calmly why she would tell my child that. Mother in law said that I did hurt her husband and it isn't up for discussion.

This is why I think I might be an asshole. I ran after her and screamed that if she had a valid reason, she would say it and walking away proves that she doesn't have a reason. Mother in law didn't answer and just calmly walked away, which obviously made me look like an ass in front of the guests. I apologised to the cousin before we left, but she seemed mad at me. My husband says it's fine and Mother in law should not have spoken to our daughter.

So am I the Asshole

70. THE SINGING FRIENDS

My friend is a good singer, I'm not denying that. But Her tone is lighter and breathier. Her range is on the higher side. And she has a softer voice not a loud big voice. People usually praise this as it's "unique" and "angelic" often referred to if that helps explain it. She can sing low notes, but I'd compare her to Ariana Grande.

We were singing along to a piano and during her part she got a bit quiet. I made a joke about how it would be helpful if she could actually learn how to use her chest voice since she didn't really have one. I also proved how it would be easier for her if she had a voice like mine, since I have a strong musical theatre voice.

She responded she naturally has a softer voice naturally and different voices have different strengths. So, I suggested if she can't do it just give me her part. The other girls then butted in, as they do, and said not everyone has to have the same voice type and that different sounds make the group sound interesting. They also said that singing loud doesn't mean singing good (apparently) and she sounded loud enough just a in mixed not full chest and apparently it sounded good.

After some practise I started to get frustrated. The part needed a clear strong voice, not a breathy whisper voice. It's just what's best for the group and our success at the audition. So, I voiced this and suggested I take her part since I don't think she suited the song.

One of the girls said in a rude tone "if you're going to dictate what everyone has to sound like and act so up your own ass that anyone who doesn't sound like you is wrong just get the fuck out" so I just left.

I tried to work things out with them later on, but they informed me they'd redistributed my solos and no longer wanted me in the group. I found this hurtful since I had everyone's best interest in mind and never said she couldn't sing. I don't see what I did wrong.

So am I the asshole?

71.THE RESTAURANT REQUIREMENTS

This sounds bad but hear me out. My stepdaughter is an absolute pain in the neck when it comes to food. She has legitimate and not mild allergies, but most of them aren't common things, so every single meal at a restaurant, no matter what she would get, would need several modifications. With so many special requests, something is always going to be wrong. I understand that, my wife understands that, and probably on some level she does too, but it is an entire event every time.

She ends up acting like the restaurant is personally trying to kill her. She, of course, has to send it back, but spirals into a breakdown and won't eat anything that they bring back anyway because it "isn't safe", regardless of what the truth is anymore. It makes the entire meal a nightmare for everyone, including the restaurant workers. The younger kids end up having their food go cold because they can't eat with the drama going on and they don't know what to do.

I finally broke and told her and my wife, while we were all together as a family, that she would just have to stop getting food when we went out and that she needs to just wait until we get home. Restaurants don't like having people bring outside food, I think it looks really rude anyway, and she just eats later at home anyway due to these episodes.

Not only that, but it is expensive as hell for her to do this. Basic meals that would comply are already not cheap, and it creates so much food waste, which I absolutely hate. My wife says that I don't understand what it's like to have to navigate food when you can't "just deal with it" like everyone else and a slight mistake can land you in the hospital, and that this makes her feel like she's less than and not part of the family. I just want to stop wasting money and food and have more quiet meals.

So am I the asshole?

72. THE ACCIDENT

So, recently, my 2 kids (14female and 6male) and I went to the store to pick up some things. It was a short trip, only meant to be 10-20 minutes, so I didn't tell my 6-year-old to go to the toilet beforehand.

The reason I had to bring my kids was because my husband works pretty much the entire day and only gets home at around 7 if he's insanely lucky. I'm just including this for context. Now, I get to the store, and after around 5 minutes, my son has an accident. There's a small puddle, not too big, but definitely noticeable, the smell is also not avoidable.

Now, the store isn't too big, so the employees and some other customers immediately notice, and begin to look at me expectantly. I apologised and began to usher my kids out of there. One of the employees tried to stop me, but I told him in no uncertain terms that my kids were embarrassed, and they were my first priority. We live in a small town, with only one school, so if word gets around, my daughter's social life could take a hit, and my son is covered in his own piss. They're my first priority, not preventing an employee from having to do something he doesn't like.

A couple of days later, everyone in the town knows, and is calling me an asshole. People are thankfully not insulting my daughter at school, but they're all saying I should have cleaned up my son's piss, and that they're never going to invite me or my son over to their homes again, because "clearly your son isn't toilet trained and you won't have the decency to clean up when he has an accident".

I can't help but feel bad because now everyone's ganging up on me. On one hand I do think it is within reason for a mother to put her kids first, but on the other hand, I understand why everyone's so angry.

So am I the Asshole?

73.THE AVID READER

Brief intro to the situation- My daughter is 22, she has a steady (but starter) job in her preferred field and rents her own place. I'm very proud of her and she's always been a great kid.

She's been back home with us for a few weeks because of the holidays, and I've noticed she reads, a LOT.

She works from home, and whenever she has breaks at work (in between calls, etc) she reads. She reads before going to sleep. She reads on weekends. She reads on car rides. Etc. She spends pretty much all of her free time reading.

She's always loved reading, but she's doing it too much recently. And it's all fiction novels - not one book for her university studies (she's a one-time dropout, trying for a second time now).

I get that it's a hobby but it's basically wasting her time, it's not really going to give her anything.

I've told her multiple times to waste less of her time, but she always just shrugs it off.

Yesterday I was driving her somewhere and we were chatting in the car, and the topic of books came up. She started talking about some fantasy mystery novel (her favourite genre) she's reading and how she basically read all of the good fantasy mystery novels in English she could find, so she started reading ones translated from Chinese.

I tried not to say anything at first, because she was so excited over it and I didn't want to ruin her excitement, but then I sort of realised I needed to intervene.

I started talking to her about how she needs to read less and focus on university more. She tried to change the topic. I pointed out that instead of reading a billion novels each week, she could take half of that time and use it to study for university, or for anything else that's not just time thrown away (like a sport, etc).

The talk escalated a bit and she got really upset, saying how reading is the only hobby she has time for these days (she used to have other hobbies, like video games, gardening, etc).

But it just doesn't make sense to me why she has to read so MUCH. I'm not telling her to stop reading altogether, just to read less.

She kept insisting that she doesn't spend that much time reading; she just consumes books very quickly, making it seem like she's reading a lot. But honestly? That's just an excuse.

In the end, what happened is that she's now upset and doesn't want to talk to me. Her dad thinks I shouldn't be interfering in what she spends her time on as she's an adult, but I still think she needed that wakeup call.

So am I the asshole?